Latimer Study 85

# ANGLICAN ELDERS?

## LOCALLY SHARED PASTORAL LEADERSHIP IN ENGLISH ANGLICAN CHURCHES

ED MOLL

The Latimer Trust

Published by the Latimer Trust May 2018

The Latimer Trust (formerly Latimer House, Oxford) is a conservative Evangelical research organisation within the Church of England, whose main aim is to promote the history and theology of Anglicanism as understood by those in the Reformed tradition. Interested readers are welcome to consult its website for further details of its many activities.

The Latimer Trust

London N14 4PS UK

Registered Charity: 1084337

Company Number: 4104465

Web: www.latimertrust.org

E-mail: administrator@latimertrust.org

## Contents Page

## Table of Figures

# Introduction

The case for changing the pattern of local leadership in Anglican churches away from a solo pastorate towards the concept of a ministry leadership team is growing. While such a change breaks with historic practice, it need not be un-Anglican. Indeed a case can be made that this is a legitimate development of Anglican principles adapted to a new missionary situation and that because the context has changed, the practice of ministry must adapt. If the church sticks with the status quo it runs the risk of becoming ineffective in post-Christendom Britain, of failing to care for the clergy themselves, and of falling short of an informed response to the New Testament patterns of local leadership.

The purpose of this study is to explore how some UK Anglican evangelical churches have put a plural leadership into practice, and how they understand the development in the light of their denominational convictions. The first three Chapters outline the biblical and historical context. A fourth Chapter summarises the findings of interviews with nine pastors, leading to practical proposals for the implementation of locally shared pastoral leadership in Anglican churches. The specific focus has been on the impact for the ministry of making disciples, that is on personal ministry rather than on aspects of corporate governance. The shepherding ministry is in fact fundamental to the wider dimensions of pastoral leadership, and provides a helpful starting point for those wishing to learn more about collaborative leadership in the local Anglican setting.

## I. From Christendom to Post-Christendom

The Church of England inherited a pattern of ministry in which the clergy minister alone. This particular legacy survived the Reformation unscathed in England and the solo pastorate has now been the normal pattern for so long that to change from it seems to involve a departure from Anglican principle as well as from historic practice. Yet Anglicanism has always been responsive to context, and the current UK context is now significantly different to the Christendom environment in which the Church of England took its first faltering steps. Indeed, as the UK moves to a post-Christendom and post-Christian society, the weaknesses of the solo pastorate become more pronounced.

During Christendom, the Church naturally occupied a position of established influence and enjoyed privilege, control, and dominance in the life of the nation. It seemed natural in the circumstances for the Church to base its identity and mission on what a recent Church of England report calls a 'come to us' strategy,[1] and a single clergyman in a parish might have seemed sufficient to manage the work in a parish of a few hundred souls. Sadly the evangelical history of the Church in England is one of dark periods punctuated by the ministries of men such as Richard Baxter (during the Commonwealth), John Wesley, Charles Whitefield, Charles Simeon and J C Ryle, which shine as lights in the spiritual gloom. Yet we note that all of these men remained committed to the principle of clerical leadership, that is the solo pastorate. Perhaps that still seemed adequate within Christendom.

Today Christendom no longer holds sway. In Great Britain the shift from a Christian to post-Christian culture is marked. Stuart Murray, a church planter and trainer, describes post-Christendom as "the culture that emerges as the Christian faith loses coherence within a society that has been definitively shaped by the Christian story and as the institutions

---

[1] Church of England, *Mission-Shaped Church: Church Planting and Fresh Expressions of Church in a Changing Context* (London: Church House Publishing, 2004), p. 11.

that have been developed to express Christian convictions decline in influence."[2] He goes on to list seven transitions that mark this shift: Christian churches have moved from the centre to the margins of society. Christians have gone from being in the majority to the minority, from settlers to sojourners because they no longer feel at home in the culture. As the culture becomes more diverse, Christians transition from privilege to plurality where Christians' privileges are eroded; from control to witness as the church's direct influence through control gives way to the indirect influence of witness; from maintenance to mission because the illusion of maintaining a Christian status quo has been shattered; and from institution to movement.[3]

Murray's analysis rings true. For instance, the 2011 population census reveals that the overall proportion of the population saying they were 'Christian' fell from seventy-two percent in England and Wales in 2001 to fifty-nine percent in 2011; the percentage saying that they had 'No Religion' rose from fifteen percent to twenty-five percent in the same time.[4] In 2013 just ten percent of the UK population were church members, and church attendance was less than half that figure.[5] Not only has the proportion calling themselves 'Christian' fallen, so has the number considering itself to be 'Anglican': just eighteen percent of the UK would consider themselves to be 'Anglican.'[6] The 'come to us' strategy is bound to fail if, as recent census data show, the bulk of the population does not even consider itself to be Anglican. The Church of England report, *Mission-Shaped Church*, is correct in stating that Britain is a post-Christendom culture in which "the Christian story is no longer

---

[2] Murray, Stuart, *Post-Christendom: Church and Mission in a Strange New World* (Carlisle: Paternoster, 2004), p. 19.

[3] Murray, *Post-Christendom*, p. 19ff. Cited also by Timmis, Steve, & Tim Chester, *Everyday Church: Mission By Being Good Neighbours* (Nottingham: IVP, 2011), pp. 21- 22.

[4] Peter Brierley, 'Geography, Christians and Those With No Religion', *Future First,* 34 (2014): 2, accessed October 10, http://www.brierleyconsultancy.com/s/510217_FUTURE_FIRST_Issue-34.

[5] Peter Brierley, 'Church Attendance', *Future First,* 33 (2014): 2, accessed October 10, 2016, http://www.brierleyconsultancy.com/s/508632_FUTURE_FIRST_Issue-33.

[6] Peter Brierley, 'UK Religion', *Future First,* 30 (2013): 2-3 accessed October 7, 2016, http://www.brierleyconsultancy.com/s/ff30.pdf Note these figures are for England, Wales and Scotland.

at the heart of the nation."[7] If a sole presbyterate was barely adequate for mission in Christendom, how can it be sufficient to meet the demands of mission in a post-Christian society? We need missionaries, and not mere chaplains to the flock.

The burden on the clergy themselves has also grown with the size and complexity of the parishes they serve. In a culture that does not want to know Christ, is less amenable to the exercise of authority, and is more resistant to challenge, the emotional demands of ministry are greater than ever before. A generation ago, David Watson already wrote that no single person could be expected to fulfil all the duties of the presbyter, and that a team was needed because

> The role of an elder is a demanding and challenging one: he is to lead, to teach, to work hard, to set an example, to tend the flock of God, to encourage, to pray for the sick, to have authority over others and to exercise discipline, to evangelise and to be well thought of by outsiders.[8]

We will see that specific areas of difficulty arise from the emotional costs of managing conflict and of exercising pastoral discipline within the church. Shared leadership offers the possibility of vital care for the ordained leaders who are otherwise left to bear their pastoral burdens in isolation, sometimes with disastrous consequences first for themselves and then for the flock.

A third and arguably even more significant call for change comes from the need to take proper account of the Scriptural data. John Stott is not alone among Anglicans in observing that, "There is no biblical warrant for the so-called one-man band, in which a single pastor, like a single musician, plays all the instruments."[9] And David Watson stated nearly thirty years earlier, "No one can claim that the familiar picture of the parish priest, working faithfully but single-handed in, say, a parish of

---

[7] Church of England, *Mission-Shaped Church*, p. 11.

[8] Watson, David, *I Believe in the Church* (London: Hodder & Stoughton, 1978), p. 272.

[9] Stott, John R. W., *The Living Church: The Convictions of a Lifelong Pastor* (Nottingham: Inter-Varsity Press, 2007), p. 81. See also Motyer, Alec, *The Message of James: The Tests of Faith* (Leicester: Inter-Varsity Press, 2000), p. 189.

20,000, comes anywhere near the rich concept of Christian ministry put forward in the New Testament."[10] Both these men were incumbents in the Church of England yet noted the New Testament pattern of shared leadership. It is not a matter of uncritically reproducing a New Testament pattern because it is there: the reasons for considering plural leadership to be more biblical will be explored below, and are that it provides a better social context for the Jesus-like exercise of pastoral leadership.

There are specific challenges for Anglicans in implementing locally shared pastoral leadership. First, and given the consistent role of history in favouring a sole pastorate, how could a plural local leadership be considered to be Anglican? The phrase plural *local* leadership is deliberately chosen to reflect that in this model leadership is shared within the local church in order to gain benefits that cannot be delivered by collaboration within the deanery, archdeaconry, episcopal area or diocese. A second challenge comes from attempts to accommodate local leaders with the established lay offices of Churchwardens and PCC members. The new structure must either find a way to colonise existing structures, or come into direct conflict with them.

The next chapters therefore begin with a survey of the relevant New Testament passages on local church leadership, before considering how the Anglican evangelical understanding of ministry arises from them. They provide the basis on which to interpret the findings of interviews with nine pastors who shared the benefits they experienced of locally shared leadership. A final chapter will outline some possible practical solutions.

## A Note on Terminology

In this study, the term elder will be preferred either to translate the Greek word *prebuteros* and deacon for *diakonos* or to describe those functions in general terms. Ordained church leaders are named presbyter rather than priest except in quotations. Pastor and minister are used interchangeably to describe the senior minister of a church.

The terms Churchwarden and Warden are synonymous.

---

[10] Watson, *I Believe in the Church*, p. 245.

A lay elder is a member of an identified Ministry Leadership Team, although individual churches may use different names for that position.

A Ministry Leadership Team (MLT) is a group of suitably qualified persons who are recognised by the church as those who share shepherding leadership with the incumbent.

Collaborative ministry (CM) and collaborative leadership (CL) are sometimes used interchangeably in sources but in this study collaborative ministry means that every member of the body is to exercise ministry for the common good, while collaborative leadership refers only to church leadership that is carried out in a collaborative or plural way.

## 2. The New Testament Background

### Elders, Overseers, Shepherds, Leaders

The key words to describe those in church leadership in the New Testament are elder (*presbuteros*), overseer (*episkopos*) and shepherd (*poimēn*). Two further terms of note are the participles describing those who lead, *hoi proïstamenoi* and *hoi hēgoumenōn*. This chapter will briefly review the main passages in which these words occur, and comment on their contribution to the plural and collaborative nature of local pastoral leadership.

Elder (*presbuteros*) and words from the same root occur in seventy-three verses of the New Testament, and refer variously to people who are older, to ancestors of the Hebrew nation, to lay Jewish leaders, to the heavenly elders,[11] and to Christian leaders.[12] Christian elders appear without introduction in Acts 11:30; C K Barrett wrote, "It is assumed, without explanation, that they exist and that they are leading members of the churches." [13] Second, elders are found in widespread churches, namely in Jerusalem;[14] in Lystra, Iconium, and Antioch;[15] in Ephesus;[16] in the towns of Crete;[17] among Peter's readers in Asia;[18] and among the recipients of James, wherever they might be.[19] Third, they are mentioned in the plural in each case except for the author of 2 John and 3 John who

---

[11] Older persons: Luke 1:18, 15:25; John 8:9; Acts 2:17; Philemon 9; 1 Timothy 5:1– 2; Titus 2:2–3; Hebrew ancestors: Matthew 15:2; Mark 7:3, 5; Hebrews 11:2; Lay Jewish leaders: Matthew 16:21; 21:23; 26:3, 47, 57; 27:1, 3, 12, 20, 41; 28:12; Mark 8:31; 11:27; 14:43, 53; 15:1; Luke 7:3; 9:22; 20:1; 22:52, 66; Acts 4:5, 8, 23; 6:12; 22:5; 23:14; 24:1; 25:15; Heavenly elders: Revelation 4:4, 10; 5:5–6, 8, 11, 14; 7:11, 13; 11:16; 14:3; 19:4.

[12] Christian leaders: Acts 11:30; 14:23; 15:2, 4, 6, 22–23; 16:4; 20:17; 21:18; 1 Timothy 4:14; 5:17, 19; Titus 1:5; James 5:14; 1 Peter 5:1, 5; 2 John 1; 3 John 1.

[13] Barrett, C. K., *Church, Ministry and Sacraments in the New Testament* (Exeter: Paternoster, 1985), p. 52.

[14] Acts 11:30; 15:2,4,6,22,23; 16:4; 21:18.

[15] Acts 14: 23.

[16] Acts 20:17, 1 Timothy 5:17, 19.

[17] Titus 1:5.

[18] 1 Peter 5:1,2 cf. 1:1.

[19] James 5:14.

introduces himself as 'the elder.'[20] F. F. Bruce suggests that the latter "was given the affectionate and respectful title 'the elder' both because he was older than the other members of the circle and because his personal knowledge of The Way went back so much farther than theirs."[21]

Eldership is often distinguished from the office of deacon (*diakonos*). Although the latter Greek word has a general meaning of 'servant,' it clearly applies to an office in 1 Timothy 3:8-13 which lists qualifications for those appointed to the office.[22] Philippians 1:1 addresses the letter to the overseers (*episkopoi*) and deacons (*diakonoi*). In Acts 6:1-6, the Seven are appointed to free up the Twelve from the need to serve (*diakonein*) at tables, but are never called 'deacons.' It may be that this passage introduces the office of deacon in the church because, unlike that of elder, it was unknown in Judaism.[23] Roger Beckwith disagrees. He notes that although the appointment of the Seven has been seen as the start of the diaconate since the time of Irenaeus, in Acts 11:30 it is presbyters who have responsibility for poor relief. In Beckwith's view the Seven were the first elders to be appointed in the church, as opposed to those who inherited the role from the synagogue.[24]

Elders are also to be overseers: both Paul's speech to the Ephesian elders at Miletus (Acts 20:18-35) and the teaching to elders in 1 Peter 5:1-4 combine the vocabulary of eldership (*presbut-*) with that of oversight (*episkop-*): the elders at Miletus are told to 'Pay careful attention to yourselves and to all the flock, of which the Holy Spirit has made you overseers (*episkopois*)'[25] while Peter urges the elders to be 'exercising oversight' (*episkopountes*).[26] Other occurrences of the *episkop-* root affirm that the terms for elder and overseer are used interchangeably: in Titus 1:5-9, the apostolic delegate is given instructions to appoint elders

---

[20] 2 John 1; 3 John 1.

[21] Bruce, F. F., *The Epistles of John* (London: Pickering & Inglis, 1970), p. 136.

[22] The reference to 'their wives' (*gunaikas*) in verse 11 may refer either to deacons' wives or to 'women' that is, female deacons. Thus ESV margin.

[23] Joseph Barber Lightfoot, 'The Christian Ministry', *Saint Paul's Epistle to the Philippians: A Revised Text With Introduction, Notes, and Dissertations* (12th edn, London: Macmillan, 1898), p. 189.

[24] Beckwith, Roger, *Elders in Every City: The Origin and Role of the Ordained Ministry* (Carlisle: Paternoster Press, 2003), pp. 42-44.

[25] Acts 20:28.

[26] 1 Peter 5:2.

(*presbuteroi*) in every town, and given a list of character qualifications for those overseers (*episkopoi*). Timothy is given a similar list for those who aspire to oversight (*episkopē*) in 1 Timothy 3.1-7; finally, the letter to the Philippians is addressed to the overseers (*episkopoi*) and deacons, in contrast to other letters which are addressed to the whole church.[27] Joseph Hellerman, Professor of New Testament language and literature at Talbot School of Theology, Biola University states, "The most straightforward way to interpret our New Testament evidence for positions of church leadership takes 'overseer' (Greek *episkopos*) as interchangeable with the more familiar 'elder' (Greek *presbuteros*), a Greek term for church leaders occurring elsewhere in Acts and the epistles (Acts 14:23; 20:17; Titus 1:5; James 5:14; 1 Peter 5:1)."[28] In this he follows a tradition stretching back at least as far as Bishop Lightfoot.[29]

The terms for shepherd (*poimēn*) and elder (*presbuteros*) also overlap: the elders of the church in Ephesus are charged to 'care for (*poimainein*) the church of God'[30] which is also described as the flock (*poimnion*) of which the Holy Spirit has made them overseers (*episkopois*).[31] Peter teaches the elders of his churches to 'shepherd the flock of God that is among you, exercising oversight (*episkopountes*)';[32] the verb is *poimanate*, a second person plural imperative. Once again, the references to the local church leaders as shepherds addresses them as a collective. The pastoral metaphor is also found in Ephesians 4:11 in which the gifts of the ascended Christ are given to, among others, 'pastors and teachers' (*poimenas kai didaskalous*). Christ himself is the ultimate Shepherd and the Overseer of our souls.[33] The theme of leader as shepherd has a long biblical pedigree, as Timothy Laniak demonstrates

---

[27] Philippians 1:1.
[28] Hellerman, Joseph, *Embracing Shared Ministry: Power and Status in the Early Church and Why it Matters Today* (Grand Rapids, MI: Kregel, 2013), p. 127. Cf. also p. 193.
[29] Joseph Barber Lightfoot, 'Excursus: The Synonymes 'Bishop' and 'Presbyter'", *Saint Paul's Epistle to the Philippians: A Revised Text With Introduction, Notes, and Dissertations* (12th edn, London: Macmillan, 1898): pp. 95-99.
[30] Acts 20:28.
[31] Acts 20:28, 29.
[32] 1 Peter 5:2.
[33] Hebrews 13:20, 1 Peter 2:25; 1 Peter 2:25, 5:4.

in his thorough biblical-theological study.[34] Thus where local church leaders are addressed in pastoral terms in the New Testament, they are addressed in the plural; only Christ the Chief Shepherd is the sole pastor of the flock.

Further terms to describe or address church leaders in the New Testament also seem to be synonymous with eldership and appear in the plural. The church in Thessalonica is urged to 'respect those who labour among you and are over you (*proïstamenous*) in the Lord and admonish you;'[35] the Hebrews are commanded to 'Remember your leaders (*hoi hēgoumenōn*), those who spoke to you the Word of God,' which probably refers to the community's now-absent founding leaders.[36] In relation to the present leadership, the church is charged to 'Obey your leaders (*tois hēgoumenois humōn*) and submit to them, for they are keeping watch over your souls, as those who will have to give an account.'[37] Finally, Romans 12:8 lists among the spiritual gifts, 'the one who leads (*ho proïstamenos*).' Although this word might also be translated 'gives aid' (so ESV margin), 'leadership' is the preferred meaning because same word occurs in connection with those who lead the Thessalonian church, and in passages describing the qualities of the elders or overseers.[38] It is to be noted that when a relationship between believers and leaders is described, the latter are listed in the plural; when the qualities of an individual leader are in view, then and only then, is the singular used.[39]

---

[34] Laniak, Timothy S, *Shepherds After My Own Heart: Pastoral Traditions and Leadership in the Bible* (Leicester: Apollos, 2006).

[35] 1 Thessalonians 5:12.

[36] Hebrews 13:7; Lane, William L., *Hebrews 9-12* (Dallas: Word Books, 1991), p. 527.

[37] Hebrews 13:17.

[38] 1 Thessalonians 5:12; 1 Timothy 3:4–5, 12; 5:17; Titus 3:8, 14. So Schreiner, Thomas R., *Romans* (Grand Rapids, MI: Baker Academic, 1998), pp. 659-660; Moo, Douglas J., *The Epistle to the Romans* (Grand Rapids, MI: Wm. B. Eerdmans, 1996), pp. 768-769.

[39] 1 Timothy 3.1-7, Titus 1.5-9 and, depending on what view is taken on translation, Romans 12:8.

## Diotrephes 'who likes to put himself first'

The sense in which *ho proïstamenos* stands out as a leader may bring to mind Diotrephes 'who likes to put himself first' (*ho philoprōteuōn*).[40] For F. F. Bruce, "The language suggests a self-appointed demagogue rather than a constitutional *presbuteros* or *episkopos*."[41] Diotrephes' actions in refusing to welcome the brothers and in putting out of the church those who would want to welcome the brothers imply an actual exercise of authority.[42] In other words, Diotrephes has assumed authority, and he is misusing it. Karen Jobes comments that 'loves to be first' (*ho philoprōteuōn*) occurs only here in the New Testament, "but the cognate adjective *philoprōtos* is found more widely in Greek writings in the sense of loving to lead by controlling others. This stands in sharp contrast to Jesus' teaching that the one who wishes to be first must be servant of all (Matthew 20:27; Mark 9:35; 10:44)."[43] She concludes, "We don't know if Diotrephes was a rightly ordained leader of the church or just a member with a forceful personality, but it hardly matters. Motivation for leadership borne from a need for control over others is always destructive in a church community and ordination is no excuse for it."[44] That Diotrephes was a forceful leader seems clear; whether he was the only leader, or whether he was failing to lead with fellow-elders cannot be determined from the text because it is not about them: it is about him and his egocentric lust for power, which he had confused with zeal for the gospel.[45] In a related context, Vanhoozer and Strachan comment that, "It is important not to confuse 'overseeing' with 'lording it over.' Peter explicitly cautions church leaders against imitating worldly leaders who abuse their power or role (1 Pet 5:3)."[46]

---

[40] 3 John 9.

[41] Bruce, *The Epistles of John*, p. 152.

[42] 3 John 10; Brown, Raymond E., *The Epistles of John* (Garden City, NY: Doubleday, 1982), p. 717.

[43] Jobes, Karen H., *1, 2, and 3 John* (Grand Rapids, MI: Zondervan, 2014), p. 313. The Greek has been transliterated.

[44] Jobes, *1, 2, and 3 John*, p. 313.

[45] Smalley, Stephen S., *1, 2, 3 John* (Revised edn, Nashville: Thomas Nelson, 2009), p. 342.

[46] Vanhoozer, Kevin J., & Owen Strachan, *The Pastor as Public Theologian: Reclaiming a Lost Vision* (Grand Rapids, MI: Baker Academic, 2015), p. 144. This section was authored by Vanhoozer.

## Plurality as a Social Context

In this connection, Hellerman sees the example of Christ in Philippians 2:6 as providing the model of leadership that draws away from status and privilege. He argues that Paul "intentionally subverts the social values of the dominant culture in the Roman colony at Philippi in order to create a radically different relational environment among the Philippians Christians."[47] In contrast to the dominant Roman honour culture and its preoccupation with status and privilege, the Philippian church was to be a place where the honour game was off-limits, a community in which persons with power and authority use their social capital not to further their own personal or familial agendas, but to serve their brothers and sisters in Christ.[48] Can such an attitude be sustained? "What was needed to guarantee that Jesus' example would become a reality among the Philippians was a social context — a way of doing church — that would encourage a Jesus-like use of authority on the part of leaders and others with status in the Philippian church." And that context is a plural leadership.[49]

Although Paul gave the family as his model for church life in Philippi, he did not follow this through by uncritically adopting the culturally normal leadership structure. "Families in the ancient world universally functioned under the aegis of strong one-man leadership, in the person of the family patriarch."[50] Instead, the church was to be led in plurality. Hellerman comments, "From what we can tell, for example, none of Paul's congregations had a solitary (or 'senior') pastor figure. All were led by a plurality of overseers. And Paul modelled team leadership in his own life and ministry, as well, partnering with Timothy, Silas, and others to spread the gospel throughout the Roman Empire." [51] Hellerman's argument is that plural leadership is biblical, not because the New Testament gives a prescription for church polity, but because the plurality approach offers much hope for raising up healthy, effective

---

47 Hellerman, *Embracing Shared Ministry*, p. 11.
48 Hellerman, *Embracing Shared Ministry*, p. 106.
49 Hellerman, *Embracing Shared Ministry*, pp. 169-170.
50 Hellerman, *Embracing Shared Ministry*, p. 194.
51 Hellerman, *Embracing Shared Ministry*, p. 193.

pastoral leaders and for significantly curbing authority abuse in churches.[52]

## Teamwork and Apostolic Delegates

Paul's example of choosing Timothy and Silas as co-workers invites a brief reflection on the nature of teamwork in other areas of biblical leadership. Aubrey Malphurs notes that while he cannot find any passage that commands believers to work in teams, it is effectively modelled throughout the Old and New Testaments. He cites the examples of Moses and his fellow judges, Jesus and his disciples, Paul with Barnabas, Mark, Silas, and Timothy, and Paul's use of the body metaphor in 1 Corinthians.[53] It may be asked whether these and other often-cited examples are instances of people functioning in teams, or in groups. For example, although Moses delegated decisions to the lesser judges, the harder cases were his alone, as anointed leader; so also in the cases of Moses with Aaron and Joshua, David and fellow heroes, and Jesus and the Twelve there is no hint of parity between the leader and his fellows such as one would expect in a team.[54] Thus up to Pentecost at least, the biblical examples of teams would be better described as a group operating under a gifted leader rather than a team functioning in a collaborative way. By contrast, the leaders of the New Testament churches are addressed as a unity, with no apparent leader among them. Letters are addressed either to churches or to individuals.

From these data alone, it might seem that up to Pentecost, team leadership in the Bible meant a strong, anointed leader supported by the people he chose, and that after Pentecost, leadership as a team would refer to elders acting as a collective of equals.[55] This structure, however, does not take account of the apostles and their delegates, who display signs of both parity and primacy. In Acts, decisions are reached and

---

[52] Hellerman, *Embracing Shared Ministry*, p. 266.

[53] Moses: Exodus 18; Jesus' disciples: Mark 3:13-19; 6:7; Paul and coworkers: Acts 11:25-26; 13:2-3, 5; 15:40; 16:1-3; The body: 1 Corinthians 12:12-31. Cited in Malphurs, Aubrey, *Advanced Strategic Planning: A 21st Century Model for Church and Ministry Leaders* (3rd edn, Grand Rapids, MI: Baker Books, 2013), p. 210.

[54] Exodus 17:10; 18.13-26; 2 Samuel 23:8-39; Mark 3:13-19.

[55] We might add, under the anointed leadership of the ascended Lord Jesus ruling through his Word and by His Spirit.

communicated by 'the apostles and elders' of the church in Jerusalem;[56] yet Peter and Paul emerge as key figures in Acts. And while Paul gathers co-workers around him, he is the lead missionary. A word study suggests that he took over from Barnabas because the order 'Barnabas and Paul' gives way to 'Paul and Barnabas.'[57] What of Paul's apostolic delegates Timothy, Titus, Erastus, and Epaphras, sent to churches on his behalf?[58] Bishop Lightfoot, in a dissertation arguing that episcopacy arose universally within two centuries of the close of the New Testament, asserts that the delegates acted as a link between the apostle's general authority and the elders' particular responsibility for the church in a particular place.

> ...with less permanence but perhaps with greater authority, the position occupied by these delegates nevertheless fairly represents the functions of the bishop early in the second century. They were in fact the link between the Apostle whose superintendence was occasional and general and the bishop who exercised a permanent supervision over an individual congregation.[59]

It is worth noting in passing that non-Anglican evangelical readers differ on how to read these data. On the one hand, Alexander Strauch's plea for a return to the New Testament pattern of plural local church leadership considers neither the apostolic delegates nor James to be local church pastors in the traditional sense.[60] He does not allow them as exceptions to the rule that local church leadership in the New Testament was always plural. On the other, Gene Getz is convinced of the need for a primary leader. He does not point to a specific text, but a perspective from the whole Bible:

---

[56] Acts 15:2, 4, 6, 22–23; 16:4.

[57] Acts 11:30; 12:25; 13:2, 7; 14:14; 15:12, 25 cf. Acts 15:2, 4, 6, 22–23; 16:4.

[58] 1 Timothy 1:1-3, Titus 1:5, Acts 19:22, Colossians 1:7.

[59] Lightfoot, *The Christian Ministry*, p. 199.

[60] Strauch, Alexander, *Biblical Eldership: An Urgent Call to Restore Biblical Church Leadership* (Revised and expanded edn, Littleton, CO: Lewis and Roth Publishers, 1995), p. 105. He adds that even if the messengers (*aggeloi*) of the churches in Revelation 2:1, 8, 12, 18; 3:1, 7, 14 are human rather than angelic, "the reference still doesn't disclose ...whether or not the representatives are the sole leaders of their local churches."

It's God's design – from the time He chose men like Moses, Joshua, Samuel, and Nehemiah in the Old Testament, and Peter, Paul, Timothy, and Titus in the New Testament – to always have a key leader in place to lead his people. Why would we think differently when it involves elders/overseers in a local church?[61]

He points to the emergence of Peter with John, and then Paul, as primary leaders among the apostles; among missionary teams, it was 'Paul and his companions'; in Jerusalem, it was 'James and the elders at Jerusalem;' in a similar way Timothy and Titus were primary leaders in the churches they served. [62] Both Getz and Strauch would formally espouse the Regulative Principle's view that the New Testament prescribes a pattern for local church leadership, yet disagree on exactly what that pattern looks like. By contrast Vanhoozer, also formally committed to the Regulative Principle, can write

The Reformers were somewhat flexible as to the exact form that church government could take. However, they agreed, first, that some order was necessary; second, that Christ has instituted the basic office of overseer; and third, that whatever form of order was decided on, it must not be set against the royal priesthood. Rather, church order and church offices exist to serve the congregation. The authority of church leaders is ministerial.[63]

## The Church and the Congregations

Another question arises when a church has more than one congregation in a given town: what does 'the church' in the place mean? Getz notes that the Greek word for church, *ekklēsia*, is used over a hundred times in the New Testament. When it refers to a church, it may either refer to the

---

[61] Getz, Gene A., *Elders and Leaders: God's Plan for Leading the Church: A Biblical, Historical, and Cultural Perspective* (Chicago: Moody Publishers, 2003), p. 223.

[62] Getz, *Elders and Leaders*, p. 223.

[63] Vanhoozer, Kevin J., *Biblical Authority After Babel: Retrieving the Solas in the Spirit of Mere Protestant Christianity* (Kindle edn, Grand Rapics, MI: Brazos Press, 2016), location 4590.

universal church or to the church in a locality.[64] According to Getz, the biblical authors use the word *ekklēsia* to refer to all the believers in a community and not simply to a congregation:

> In most instances, New Testament writers were referring to all professing believers in a particular *city* or *community*. Luke cited "the church at *Jerusalem*" (Acts 8:1) and "the church at *Antioch*" (13:1). Describing Paul's first missionary journey, Luke references "each church" in "*Lystra, Iconium* and *Antioch* [Pisidia]" (14:21-23).[65]

Getz' point is that 'the church' is a church in a community, even if it is composed of several house-church gatherings. In a similar way, Guy Prentiss Waters, in advancing an argument for Presbyterian church government, points out that during the apostolic period the church existed in several congregations but was spoken of as 'the church' in the singular. "Meeting places for the church, Acts and the Epistles tell us, were private dwellings."[66] It seems to him reasonable to conclude that the congregations were collectively governed by the apostles and individually governed by groups of elders. Allan Chapple investigated how Paul's letter to the Romans would reach its intended audience, and concluded that Phoebe was to deliver *Romans* to a number of house churches as well as to an assembly of the whole church which would be convened by Prisca and Aquila.[67] These studies suggest that the city churches met in houses churches *and* had some sort of city-wide identity.

The differences between these writers, and more could be cited, illustrate the difficulty of distinguishing Paul's charge to Titus to appoint elders in every *town* in Crete,[68] and Paul and Barnabas' actions in

---

[64] Except in Acts 7:38 where *ekklēsia* refers to the community of Israel gathered in the wilderness and in Acts 19:32 to the riot in Ephesus and in 19:39 to the 'regular assembly' of that city.

[65] Getz, *Elders and Leaders*, p. 49. Emphasis original.

[66] Waters, Guy Prentiss, *How Jesus Runs the Church* (Phillipsburg, NJ: P & R Publishing, 2011), p. 123. For recent challenge to the consensus that Christians met only in homes, see Adams, Edward, *The Earliest Christian Meeting Places: Almost Exclusively Houses?* (London: Bloomsbury T & T Clark, 2013).

[67] Allan Chapple, 'Getting Romans to the Right Romans: Phoebe and the Delivery of St Paul's Letter', *Tyndale Bulletin*, 62/2 (2011), p. 208.

[68] Titus 1:5.

appointing elders in every *church* in Lystra, Iconium and Antioch.[69] For Getz, however, the ambiguity is divinely ordained. "God wants believers in various cultural settings to be able to create a multiple leadership plan that will function effectively regardless of whether we live in the first century or the church of the twenty-first."[70]

## Conclusion

Taken as a whole, the New Testament data suggest that local church leadership was plural, and that elders, shepherds and overseers were synonymous. But the exact details of local church polity remain somewhat elusive. And to what extent the New Testament pattern is prescriptive depends on how these biblical data are to be read and understood.

---

[69] Acts 14:23.
[70] Getz, *Elders and Leaders*, p. 211.

## 3. THE ANGLICAN EVANGELICAL UNDERSTANDING OF MINISTRY

### The Normative Principle and the Shape of Ministry

"Few branches of the Christian church", says Gerald Bray, "have as much difficulty defining themselves as the Anglican one has."[71] It follows that outlining an Anglican understanding of ministry that embraces all shades of opinion is an impossible as well as a fruitless task. For our purposes, it is enough to outline an *evangelical* Anglican understanding of ministry. Those who hold this view will be denoted 'Anglican evangelical' because their prior commitment is to evangelical ministry. There is a hierarchy, as Kevin Vanhoozer notes in commenting on Timothy George's self-description as an Evangelical and a Baptist: "it is possible for one and the same person to be, for example, a Protestant, Baptist, and evangelical, though the disciple's deepest identity is one who is 'in Christ' by the grace of the triune God."[72] In such a hierarchy, these Anglicans' deeper identity is as evangelicals.

We might at this juncture also note the distinction between 'Anglican' and 'Church of England'. In this study, 'Anglican' is the broader term and refers to a theological vision rooted in Scripture and expounded by the Formularies (The Thirty-nine Articles, the Book of Common Prayer, and the Ordinal), while 'Church of England' refers to one institutional expression of Anglicanism. The Anglican Mission in England (AMiE) would also claim to give expression to the Anglican theological vision.

The first step is to recognise the important role that history plays in Anglican evangelical self-understanding. John Stott is not alone in leaning on history in his defence of an Anglican identity on the basis that

---

[71] Gerald L. Bray, 'Why I Am an Evangelical and an Anglican', in Anthony L Chute, Christopher W Morgan, & Robert A Peterson (eds), *Why We Belong* (Wheaton, IL: Crossway, 2013), p. 65.

[72] Vanhoozer, *After Babel*, loc. 6167. He is making reference to Timothy F. George, 'Why I Am an Evangelical and a Baptist', in Anthony L Chute, Christopher W Morgan, & Robert A Peterson (eds), *Why We Belong* (Wheaton. IL: Crossway, 2013), p. 108.

the Church of England is historical, confessional and liturgical.[73] The role of history follows from the commitment of Stott and others to the Normative principle (as opposed to the Regulative principle). Since Richard Hooker is credited with first articulating this principle, the Normative is sometimes dubbed the Hooker Principle which Paul Bradshaw explains as:

> The evangelical conviction that God has provided clearly and definitely in some areas of church life, but has left others more open and flexible. The aspects in which revelation firmly operates concern salvation in Christ; the areas in which the church has a freedom to act concern the structures and customs of the church.[74]

Or by Reformed Baptist Mark Dever (an advocate for the Regulative principle):

> Briefly, the Regulative Principle states that everything we do in a corporate worship gathering must be clearly warranted by Scripture. Clear warrant can either take the form of an explicit biblical command, or a good and necessary implication of a biblical text. The Regulative Principle has historically competed with the Normative Principle, crystallized by the Anglican minister Richard Hooker.

---

[73] Stott, *The Living Church*, pp. 167-177. Similarly Bray, *Why I Am an Evangelical and an Anglican*; Gerald L. Bray, 'The Pastor as Evangelical and Anglican', in Melvin Tinker (ed.), *The Renewed Pastor: Essays on the Pastoral Ministry in Honour of Philip Hacking* (Fearn: Christian Focus, 2011): pp. 239-255; David Holloway, 'What is an Anglican Evangelical?', in Melvin Tinker (ed.), *Restoring the Vision: Anglican Evangelicals Speak Out* (Crowborough: MARC, 1990), p. 18; Turnbull, Richard, *Anglican and Evangelical?* (London: Continuum, 2007), p. 165; Alister McGrath, 'Evangelical Anglicans: A Contradiction in Terms?', in R T France, & Alister McGrath (eds), *Evangelical Anglicans: Their Role and Influence in the Church Today* (London: SPCK, 1993), p. 10; David Atkinson, 'Evangelicalism and Pastoral Ministry', in R T France, & Alister McGrath (eds), *Evangelical Anglicans: Their Role and Influence in the Church Today* (London: SPCK, 1993), pp. 152-153.; Packer (but not Wright) in Packer, J I, & N T Wright, *Anglican Evangelical Identity: Yesterday and Today* (London: Latimer Trust, 2008)

[74] Bradshaw, Timothy, *The Olive Branch: An Evangelical Anglican Doctrine of the Church* (Carlisle: Paternoster Press for Latimer House, 1992), p. 143.

Hooker argued, along with Martin Luther before him, that as long as a practice is not biblically forbidden, a church is free to use it to order its corporate life and worship. In short, the Regulative Principle forbids anything not commanded by Scripture, whereas the Normative Principle allows anything not forbidden by Scripture.[75]

Hooker's position contrasts with the Roman Catholic view in which the church's tradition is of at least equal weight to Scripture, and to the prevailing Presbyterian Puritan view that tradition should be of no weight.[76] The Normative and Regulative Principles, that is the hermeneutic employed, can make sense of why Anglican and non-Anglican evangelicals read the same New Testament data and draw differing conclusions for contemporary practice. Steve Cowan's editorial introduction to a symposium on church order between Anglican, Presbyterian, and Baptist authors explains:

> Where one comes down on the issue of church government will depend to some degree on the principles of interpretation with which one approaches the biblical text. In particular, it clearly matters whether one believes that church practices should be limited to what the Scriptures explicitly teach or command, or whether one believes that the churches are free to adopt any practice that the Scriptures do not forbid.[77]

According to the Regulative Principle, then, the New Testament provides a firm pattern to be followed. For Reformed Baptist Mark Dever, "The pattern is a plurality of elders in each local church."[78] Presbyterian Philip Ryken determines that because the biblical terms for shepherd, elder, and

---

[75] Dever, Mark, & Paul Alexander, *The Deliberate Church* (Wheaton, IL: Crossway, 2005), p. 77. Their footnote cites Carson, D. A., Mark Ashton, R. Kent Hughes, & Timothy Keller, *Worship By the Book* (Grand Rapids, MI: Zondervan, 2002), pp. 25, 54-55. which notes that in practice both the Normative and Regulative principles have stronger and weaker forms.
[76] Bradshaw, *The Olive Branch*, p. 147.
[77] Paul E Engle, & Steve B Cowan (eds), *Who Runs the Church? Four Views on Church Government* (Grand Rapids, MI: Zondervan, 2004), p. 16.
[78] Dever, & Alexander, *Deliberate Church*, p. 132.

overseer are synonymous, the biblical pattern for church leadership is one of collaboration rather than stratification:

> God does not intend for bishops to rule the pastors, who in turn govern the elders. Instead, God has invested spiritual authority in a group of men – use whichever term for them you like – who together give wise counsel, spiritual oversight, and personal care to God's people. *A Christian church has a team of shepherds who provide loving pastoral care for every member of the church family.*[79]

Guy Prentiss Waters, also writing from a Presbyterian view, follows James Bannerman's distinction between *jure humano* ('the form of government for [the] church should be left to the discretion and judgment of its members, and should be adjusted by them to suit the circumstances of the age, or country, or civil government with which they stand connected') and *jure divino* ('the form and arrangements of ecclesiastical government have not been left to be fixed by the wisdom of man, nor reduced to the level of a question of mere Christian expediency, but have been determined by Divine authority, and are sufficiently exhibited in Scripture'), and argues firmly for the latter.[80] He discerns two offices in the church, namely elders and deacons, while recognising that others have found three offices. [81] Fellow-Presbyterian Kevin Vanhoozer, however, prefers to keep the emphasis on the leaders' functions over their exact arrangement:

> Mere Protestant polity is less interested in the particulars than in the basic principle of *episkopē:* oversight. Whatever we call them – elders, presbyters, pastors, or bishops – the

---

[79] Ryken, Philip Graham, *City on a Hill: Reclaiming the Biblical Pattern for the Church in the 21st Century* (Chicago: Moody Publishers, 2003), p. 99. Emphasis original.

[80] Waters, *How Jesus Runs the Church*, pp. 42-43. He is citing Bannerman, James *The Church of Christ: A Treatise on the Nature, Powers, Ordinances, Discipline and Government of the Christian Church*, 2 vols. (London: Banner of Truth, 1960), 2:202-4.

[81] For a three-office view, see Robert S. Rayburn, 'Ministers, Elders, and Deacons', in Mark R. Brown (ed.), *Order in the Offices: Essays Defining the Roles of Church Officers* (Duncansville, PA: Classic Presbyterian Government Resources, 1993): pp. 223-227

basic task of overseers is to preserve the integrity of the church's witness to the economy of the gospel as attested in the Scriptures (and tradition).[82]

Alexander Strauch is introduced only as a gifted Bible teacher and an elder at a church in Littleton, Colorado, where he has served for over forty years. His concern in *Biblical Eldership* is to restore a biblical pattern of eldership to the church: "A true biblical eldership is not a business-like committee. It's a biblically qualified council of men that jointly pastors the local church."[83] Strauch notes the consistent use of the plural when describing elders or church leaders and finds these data conclusive. "On the local church level, the New Testament plainly witnesses to a consistent pattern of shared pastoral leadership. Therefore, leadership by a plurality of elders is a sound biblical practice."[84]

In contrast to their Regulative Principle brethren, Anglican evangelicals read the Scriptural data as giving principles rather than patterns, as Alec Motyer explains: "Within the Anglican circle at any rate there seems to be agreement that we search in vain for a pattern of ministry which we can reproduce today, and thereby claim New Testament authority for what we do."[85] An important corollary of this approach is that the implementation of these principles is expected to change according to the historical context, as Jesuit ecclesiologist Avery Dulles agrees. "A historical study of the development of Christian ministry would probably show that the church in every age has adjusted its structures and offices so as to operate more effectively in the social environment in which it finds itself."[86]

This hermeneutical digression has a point: it enables one to determine whether a move to plural local leadership is Anglican, and the answer depends on how one gets there. If plural local eldership is given as a pattern 'because the Bible says so', then it stems from a Regulative Principle reading. A nominally Anglican church adopting shared

---

[82] Vanhoozer, *After Babel*, loc. 4570.

[83] Strauch, *Biblical Eldership*, p. 31.

[84] Strauch, *Biblical Eldership*, p. 37.

[85] Alec Motyer, 'The Meaning of Ministry', in Melvin Tinker (ed.), *Restoring the Vision: Anglican Evangelicals Speak Out* (Crowborough: MARC, 1990), p. 236.

[86] Dulles, Avery, *Models of the Church* (Dublin: Gill and Macmillan, 1974), p. 152.

leadership for this reason would in fact be crypto-Baptist or crypto-Presbyterian or crypto-Congregationalist. However if plural leadership is arrived at as a legitimate historical development arising from the application of biblical principles to the current situation, then such a use of the Normative Principle would indeed be authentically Anglican. When this issue was explored with the nine participants interviewed, all came out as holding to the Normative Principle. Shared leadership is more biblical because it enables biblical practices and values better to be expressed. In Hellerman's terms, it is the social context that encourages a Jesus-like use of authority on the part of leaders and others with status in the church.[87]

## History and the shape of ministry up to the Reformation

The historical development of the ordained ministry traces how the shape of ministry has responded to a changing historical context, and explains why Anglican ministry looks like it does at a given point in time. Lightfoot showed that within the New Testament, the offices of bishop (*episkopos*) and elder (*presbuteros*) were synonymous.[88] Yet by the close of the second century, the office of bishop was separate from the presbyterate, emerging from the presbyters rather than the apostles. "The episcopate was formed not out of the apostolic order by localisation but out of the presbyteral by elevation: and the title, which originally was common to all, came at length to be appropriated to the chief among them."[89] The evidence for how this came about is fragmentary, but Lightfoot cites plentiful sources from the Fathers of the episcopate's early history and widespread adoption.[90] Vanhoozer and Strachan agree on the fact of the rise of the episcopate, but not its aetiology: "The development of what is called the 'monarchical episcopate,' the ecclesial oversight of a region by a bishop, is shrouded in some mystery, we must admit. It is not immediately clear how this system of polity came to be adopted by the

---

[87] Hellerman, *Embracing Shared Ministry*, pp. 169-170. Cited in Chapter Two above.
[88] Lightfoot, *Excursus*
[89] Lightfoot, *The Christian Ministry*, p. 196.
[90] Lightfoot, *The Christian Ministry*, pp. 208-227.

early church; there was no once-for-all decree handed down to the early church that led to the formation of this ecclesial system."[91]

As the sacerdotal view of ministry grew, so church polity hardened into three separate orders of ministry: bishops, presbyters, and deacons.[92] Beckwith states that in the face of doctrinal disputes, the Eucharist may have been focused in the hands of the bishop because of the need for church discipline, which centred on exclusion from and readmission to the Lord's Table. Putting it in the hands of the bishop prevented the excommunicated from setting up their own tables.[93] The presiding presbyter thus held the functions of directing worship, ordinations, and discipline. As the church grew, presbyters were dispersed to outlying parishes and regained some of their rights in the direction of worship and the exercise of discipline, but not in the practice of ordination.[94] A consequence of the presbyters' dispersal was that they now found themselves working alone. "Thus congregations with a sole presbyterate, instead of the plural presbyterate usual from New Testament times in the towns, became normal. The sole presbyterate afterwards spread to towns as well."[95] This is the pattern that Cranmer and Hooker inherited. While Cranmer's Ordinal reformed the purpose of the clerical ministry to one of Word and teaching, the singular nature of the presbyterate was not affected. Thanks to Hooker, clericalism, that is the sole presbyterate, survived the Reformation almost unscathed.[96]

## History and the shape of ministry since the Reformation

Cranmer departed from the inherited Sarum view of priesthood when he recovered the Church of England's ministry as one of Word and Sacrament, beginning with his 1550 Ordinal. The New Testament readings chosen for the 1550 Ordinal's ordering of Priests were Acts 20 and 1 Timothy 3, which emphasise that the ministry is one of teaching,

---

[91] Vanhoozer, & Strachan, *Pastor as Public Theologian*, p. 72. The chapter was written by Strachan.
[92] Lightfoot, *The Christian Ministry*, p. 263.
[93] Beckwith, *Elders in Every City*, p. 57.
[94] Beckwith, *Elders in Every City*, pp. 58-59.
[95] Beckwith, *Elders in Every City*, p. 77.
[96] Murray, *Post-Christendom*, p. 261.

leadership, and sanctifying, as opposed to being a sacerdotal ministry.[97] In the giving of the instruments (chalice and paten), the words of the prayer altered the traditional meaning, and in the 1552 revision, the giving of the chalice and paten was removed altogether so that only the Bible was given.[98]

Cranmer's use of the word 'priest' has troubled evangelical readers. Stott's comment may usefully be quoted:

> It may be asked why in the sixteenth century some Reformed churches retained the word 'priest' as a designation of their ministers, including the Church of England. The answer is primarily one of etymology. The English word 'priest' was known to be derived from, and a contraction of, 'presbyter.' It therefore translated *presbyteros* ('elder'), not *hierus* ('priest'). So 'priest' was kept only because its meaning was theologically unexceptionable and because 'presbyter' was not yet a word of common English currency. ... today few people know that 'priest' is a contraction of 'presbyter,' and even fewer are able to perform the mental gymnastic of saying 'priest' and thinking 'presbyter.' It would therefore be conducive to both theological clarity and biblical faithfulness to drop the word 'priest' altogether from our vocabulary. We could then follow the wisdom of such united churches as those of South India, North India, and Pakistan, and refer to the three orders of ordained ministry as 'bishops, presbyters and deacons.'[99]

In a similar vein, Vanhoozer and Strachan note that although pastors were frequently called 'priests' by the end of the second century they clearly understood themselves as teachers of the people of God. They

---

[97] Echlin, Edward P., *The Story of Anglican Ministry* (Slough: St Paul Publications, 1974), p. 90.

[98] Echlin, *Anglican Ministry*, p. 107.

[99] Stott, John R. W., *The Contemporary Christian* (Leicester: IVP, 1992), p. 274. Also the discussion of Article XXIV 'Of Speaking in the Congregation in such a Tongue as the People understandeth' in Bray, Gerald L., *The Faith We Confess: An Exposition of the Thirty-Nine Articles* (London: The Latimer Trust, 2009), p. 130.

conclude also that since for Chrysostom (347 – 407 AD) the pastor was a teacher, the pastorate was then a theological office.[100]

The role of bishops became a critical issue in the seventeenth century as attitudes to the episcopate changed. In the Elizabethan Church it had been understood as one possible form of church government, but under the Stuarts it came to be seen as a divine institution that would brook no rivals.[101] The key issue became the validity of presbyteral as opposed to episcopal ordination. Attempts by Archbishop Ussher (1581 – 1656) to reiterate that the difference between bishops and presbyters was only one of office failed to hold the day, and the backlash against the Commonwealth was so decisive that by 1662 episcopal ordination was firmly entrenched. Bradshaw notes, "The bishops had made episcopal ordination necessary *de facto*; it only remained for them to revise the Ordinal and make it necessary *de jure*, and victory over the Puritans would be complete."[102]

Most of the changes to the Ordinal for 1662 were therefore devised to exclude a Puritan interpretation of the Ordinal. Ephesians 4:7-13 replaced the Bible reading from 1 Timothy 3 because Puritans felt the latter showed bishops and presbyters belonged to the same order. The reading from Acts 20, to which Ussher had made appeal to show that the church at Ephesus was ruled by many elders in common and that the Church of England intended her presbyters to do the same under the presidency of the bishop, was dropped.[103] Finally, the word 'pastors' was removed from the rite for presbyters so that Puritans could not claim that presbyters as well as bishops were to rule their flocks. The Church of England thus set its face against all attempts to reform the presbyterate into anything resembling a Presbyterian plural eldership.

It should not be thought that all Puritans were resolutely anti-clerical. Richard Baxter, author of *The Reformed Pastor*, takes Acts 20:28's "take heed of all the flock" as his point of departure to commend

---

[100] Vanhoozer, & Strachan, *Pastor as Public Theologian*, pp. 71, 74. Strachan is the author of this section.

[101] Bradshaw, Paul F., *The Anglican Ordinal: Its History and Development From the Reformation to the Present Day* (London: SPCK for the Alcuin Club, 1971), p. 61.

[102] Bradshaw, *The Anglican Ordinal*, p. 70. Italics original.

[103] Bradshaw, *The Anglican Ordinal*, pp. 90-91.

the use of 'humiliation' and catechesis in pastoral ministry.[104] Timothy Witmer, writing from within the Presbyterian tradition and in favour of plural pastoral eldership, is struck by Baxter's reluctance to draw his fellow-elders into the work of pastoral care. "Baxter did not see the ruling elder as a key partner in the work of shepherding the flock."[105] David Sceats, Director of Local Ministry Development in the Diocese of Lichfield in the Church of England, disagrees with Baxter's high view of the ordained ministry:

> There are certainly times when, in common with his peers, the language he uses of the dignity and honour of the ministry is so exalted that it is hard to escape the conclusion that he is describing something remarkably similar in practice (if not in concept) to the priesthood he so vigorously criticises in those who espouse the 'prelatical' or 'romish' factions.[106]

Anglican evangelicals of the twentieth century have not been content to allow the 1662 Ordinal to go unchallenged. Timothy Bradshaw proposes that in place of clericalism, "teams of pastors, teachers, evangelists, carers and others, with varying complementary strengths, rather than the single bearer of that responsibility, may be the truly evangelical apostolic ideal of ministry."[107] Michael Green also wants to take a broad view of ministry as "a shared and multiple local leadership such as prevailed in the corporate presbyterate of the early church."[108]

Thus although the Church of England's local church leadership is clerical and solitary because of tradition, Anglican evangelicals are unwilling for that tradition to remain unchallenged and unchanged. Three developments in the last century added impetus to the call for

---

[104] Baxter, Richard, *The Reformed Pastor* (Edinburgh: Banner of Truth Trust, 1974).

[105] Witmer, Timothy Z, *The Shepherd Leader: Achieving Effective Shepherding in Your Church* (Phillipsburg, NJ: P & R Publishing, 2010), p. 62.

[106] David Sceats, 'Gildas Savianas Redivivus - the Reformed Pastor, Richard Baxter', *Anvil*, 10/2 (1993), pp. 140-141. Thanks to Revd. Dr Lee Gatiss for this reference.

[107] Bradshaw, *The Olive Branch*, p. 169.

[108] Green, Michael, *Freed to Serve: Training and Equipping for Ministry* (2nd edn, London: Hodder and Stoughton, 1988), pp. 93-94.

change, namely the charismatic movement, the call for women's ordination, and the liberal church's response to denominational decline.

David Watson, evangelist and vicar of St Michael-le-Belfroy in York, was a leading Anglican influenced by charismatic renewal. He was also an articulate exponent of the principle that ministry involves the whole body and not merely the 'parish priest.'[109] He proposed a return to the New Testament pattern of shared ministry and shared leadership:

> Although there might well have been a presiding elder [in the New Testament churches], there is never the slightest hint of a solitary leader (such as the vicar, the minister, the pastor), even in the smallest and youngest churches. ... Nowhere is there any suggestion of a one-man ministry except in the sad and telling comment about Diotrephes, 'who likes to put himself first.'[110]

Michael Green's suggestion cited above of shared ministry was written at a time when women could be ordained deacon but not presbyter in the Church of England.[111] At the time, then, shared leadership provided a way for women to exercise leadership and sidestep the institutional bar on their ordination as presbyters. The fruit among evangelicals of these two pressures, charismatic renewal and the ordination of women, was the mobilisation of a trained and empowered laity:

> Across the years, evangelical Anglicans have accumulated a wide experience of a trained and biblically literate laity, committed to mutual pastoral care and to evangelism. They have evidence to convince others that it actually works. At their best, evangelicals have never lost sight of the New Testament understanding that the 'servant' role of the authorized church leader is to teach others and equip the whole body of Christ to be ministers of the Gospel.[112]

---

[109] Watson, *I Believe in the Church*, p. 245.

[110] Watson, *I Believe in the Church*, p. 271. He is citing 3 John 9.

[111] Green wrote in 1988. The Church of England decided to ordain women to the presbyterate in 1994 and to the episcopate in 2014.

[112] Gillian Summers, 'Evangelicals and Patterns of Ministry', in R T France, & Alister McGrath (eds), *Evangelical Anglicans: Their Role and Influence in the Church Today* (London: SPCK, 1993), p. 163.

Non-evangelicals in the Church of England have also discovered lay leadership but for different reasons. Writing ten years after Summers, Andrew Dawswell states, "One of the most radical developments in the Church of England over recent years has been the widespread emergence of a new layer of leadership and ministry, variously termed the leadership team, pastoral team, ministry team or eldership."[113] Leslie J. Francis cites dozens of references in support of his claim that "collaborative ministry has been a major theme in church thinking, ecumenically and internationally, over the past two decades."[114] He admits that "The practical case for collaborative ministry begins with the recognition that the ageing profile of clergy, the declining vocations of full-time stipendiary ministry, the eroding economic base on which the churches operate, and the drift of the population away from church membership and church attendance all conspire to undermine the sustainability of traditional forms of ministry." Another possible motivation is the reduction of clergy stress.[115] Robin Greenwood, a leading non-evangelical exponent of collaborative ministry, gives this brief definition:

> Ministry Leadership Teams consist of those in ordained and licensed ministry and others who, together and in diversity, lead, encourage and build up the work of the whole Body of Christ. [116]

It is striking that the wider church caught up for seemingly pragmatic reasons with what evangelicals had been saying for theological reasons: that leadership should be biblical, local, plural, and adapted to local context.

Some of the developments mentioned above will resonate with reformed Anglican evangelicals. Collaborative, or every-member, ministry is an accepted implication of the Bible's teaching on spiritual

---

[113] Dawswell, Andrew, *Ministry Leadership Teams: Theory and Practice in Effective Collaborative Ministry* (Cambridge: Grove Books, 2003), p. 3.

[114] Leslie J Francis, Susan H Jones, & Mandy Robbins, 'Clergy Personality and Collaborative Ministry: The Way Ahead for Stable Extraverts?', *Pastoral Psychology*, 53/1 (2004), pp. 33-36.

[115] Francis, Jones, & Robbins, *Clergy Personality and Collaborative Ministry*, p. 35.

[116] Greenwood, Robin, *The Ministry Team Handbook* (London: SPCK, 2000), p. xi. This is cited in Dawswell, *Ministry Leadership Teams*, p. 3.

gifts, even if evangelicals differ on the nature of some of the gifts. Conservative evangelicals espousing a complementarian understanding of ministry would not be looking for ways to sidestep a barrier to women's ordination as presbyters. Within their theological commitment to a view that eldership (whether the ordained presbyterate or some form of local lay elder) should be open only to suitably qualified men, conservative and complementarian evangelicals seek other ways to bring women's voices into the pastoral conversation, as will be seen from the interview findings. And finally, the push for shared leadership as a response to decline and ageing in the church has not been a driver for change among evangelicals. In part this is because the effects of decline and ageing have not been felt as acutely among them as in other wings of the church, but mainly the impetus towards collaborative leadership has come from Scripture and from the needs of mission in a post-Christendom society.

## What is the Local Church?

It will be noted from the above that the natural unit of the church for Anglican evangelicals is the local church rather than the diocese. Watson was advocating collaborative leadership within the local church, not among the presbyters in a diocese as Ussher had suggested in the seventeenth century.

The theological conviction is that the basic unit of the church is the local congregation. The rationale is not, as some might suppose, to be found in Article XIX of the 39 Articles of Religion, which at first glance seems to identify the church with the local congregation:

XIX of the Church

The visible Church of Christ is a congregation of faithful men, in the which the pure Word of God is preached, and the sacraments be duly ministered according to Christ's ordinance in all those things that of necessity are requisite to the same.

As the Church of Jerusalem, Alexandria, and Antioch, have erred; so also the Church of Rome hath erred, not only in their living and manner of Ceremonies, but also in matters of Faith.[117]

Bray explains that the word 'congregation' is difficult. "To us it suggests a parish church, but it is doubtful whether Cranmer intended it in that sense."[118] And it is possible that 'church' here refers to what we might call a denomination. Indeed, Cranmer's mention of the great patriarchates of the ancient world suggests that he thought more in terms of national or regional churches, which were 'congregations' in the sense that they were churches because they had gathered around the Word of God. The point being made in the Article is that, as against the claims of the Church of Rome, the church is defined confessionally not institutionally.

This national sense of the congregation, that is a confessionally-defined church, finds its visible expression in the local congregation. John Woodhouse, former Principal of Moore Theological College in Sydney, states that it is in a congregation rather than a denomination that a confessional church is visible, and the Article states that the visible church of Christ is a congregation.[119] For this reason, Anglican evangelicals are oriented to the local congregation and the basic visible unit of a confessionally defined church is the local congregation. Non-Anglican Vanhoozer also places the emphasis on the local congregation when he writes that it is "in local gatherings that Jesus enacts his rule through the ministry of his word. The local church is that place where God's people gather together to make Christ's kingdom visible on earth as it is in heaven."[120] The focus of the church is the local congregation, not because Article XIX uses that word, but because it is in the local congregation that a confessional church is visible.

At a practical level, the size of English dioceses also makes genuine collaborative ministry across a diocese or even a deanery impractical as well as theologically incoherent. The Diocese of Bath and Wells, for example, has over 500 churches grouped in over 200 parishes, overseen by two bishops; and like the rest of the Church of England, this

---

[117] Article XIX 'Of the Church'.

[118] Bray, *The Faith We Confess*, p. 107.

[119] Woodhouse, John, *Unity That Helps & Unity That Hinders* (Sheffield: Reform, 2001), pp. 34-35. Emphasis added.

[120] Vanhoozer, *After Babel*, loc 4730. He draws heavily on books on church membership by Jonathan Leeman.

diocese represents a very diverse range of theological positions. In no sense can this realistically approximate even to the city-church of the New Testament. If presbyteral ministry is to be shared, it must be done locally, and this would be a departure from the historic Anglican practice that grew up in Christendom.

## Conclusion

For Anglican evangelicals, then, the ordained ministry of presbyters is one of Word and sacrament, of teaching, eldership and enabling; and the focus of that ministry is the local church. Scripture and mission impel evangelicals towards the New Testament pattern of plural ministry and leadership. The late twentieth-century movements for charismatic renewal, women's ordination, and collaborative ministry as a response to church decline have only intensified the momentum for change. But any change must take account of both the dynamics of parish life, and the existing legal structures.

## 4. FINDINGS

In order to explore the practical benefits of shared pastoral leadership in a local church, research interviews were conducted with Anglican ministers whose churches had established what we are calling a Ministry Leadership Team, although individual churches use different terminology. Nine ministers were interviewed and asked about the experience of shared leadership with respect to making disciples. Participants were drawn from the relatively small mission-oriented conservative Anglican evangelical constituency. The *UK Christian Handbook* estimates that 1,411 of 37,501 English churches are 'mainstream' evangelical, which is usually taken as conservative evangelical.[121] In personal communication the editor further estimates the number of mainstream evangelical Anglican churches in 2015 to be above 2,000.[122] However this group includes egalitarian evangelicals and the number of conservative and complementarian evangelical churches is thought to be significantly lower than the figure given. The churches led by these men divide into three groups: two are parish churches, three are proprietary chapels and four are church plants. Two of the plants and one of the parish churches meet in multiple congregations and sites. The four church plants – all Anglican – are divided between those within the Church of England and those receiving oversight from the Anglican Mission in England (AMiE). The plants are all less than fifteen years old and are each led by their founding pastor. Great care was needed to preserve the anonymity of the data, and for this reason names and occasionally terminology have been changed.[123]

The most striking finding of the research interviews was that despite their very similar theological vision for ministry, these pastors have implemented shared leadership in different ways. No single pattern predominated and no simple relationship exists between the types of church, be it parish church, proprietary chapel or church plant, and the form of leadership structure in place. There is therefore no 'right' answer

---

[121] Peter Brierley, 'Churchmanship of Churches 1989-2005', *U K Christian Handbook,* 6 (2006): Table 5.14.

[122] Peter Brierley, letter to author, June 4, 2016.

[123] See further C D E Moll, 'Anglican Elders? Shared Pastoral Leadership in Anglican Churches', D. Min. Covenant Theological Seminary, St Louis, MO (2017) especially Chapters Four and Five.

to the question of how to share local pastoral leadership in Anglican churches in order best to serve the mission of making disciples in a post-Christendom culture. Instead we may offer the following observations. First, some key principles underpin a biblically informed ministry leadership structure. Second, the pastors articulated clear benefits, echoed in the literature, arising from locally shared pastoral oversight. Third, there are practices that promote healthy collaboration between the members of the Ministry Leadership Team (MLT). Chapter Five will outline possible structures and note their advantages and disadvantages.

The focus of this research has been on the personal ministry of leaders with members of the congregation. Another name for this might be the shepherding ministry. Timothy Witmer's contention is that leaders are pictured in the Bible as shepherds, and that shepherding gives a comprehensive matrix for ministry. Vanhoozer and Strachan also look to the pastoral metaphor to elaborate on the nature of leadership within the Christian church: "The pastor, like Peter, is a shepherd, but this shepherding work is not physical with rod and staff, but spiritual, with verbs and nouns." [124] Witmer further divides the task into those aspects that concern the whole congregation, and those that are primarily focused on individuals:

> Macro-shepherding refers to important leadership functions that relate to the entire church. It has in sight the elders' responsibility to provide "oversight" to the flock as a whole. Its concern is to address the corporate concerns of the congregation. ... Micro-shepherding, on the other hand, refers to the personal ministry of the elders among the sheep. It has in view the particular sheep for whom they have been given responsibility ... The micro focus is on developing relationships with the sheep and the exercise of shepherding functions on a personal level. [125]

Establishing a Ministry Leadership Team also benefited the macro-shepherding ministry, but that is beyond the scope of the present investigation.

---

[124] Vanhoozer, & Strachan, *Pastor as Public Theologian*, p. 58.
[125] Witmer, *Shepherd Leader*, pp. 103, 104. Emphasis original. Witmer draws on Laniak, *Shepherds After My Own Heart*.

## Key Principles

The churches that established locally shared pastoral leadership did so on the basis of common principles which in turn informed the shape of their Ministry Leadership Team and its practices.

### Let the Teachers Lead

The Anglican evangelical understanding of ordination to ministry as a presbyter is that it is ordination to a ministry of the Word and of the Sacraments, as noted above in Chapter Three. We may add further that the sacraments are an extension of the ministry of the Word and that in the words of Calvin, a sacrament is a "visible word."[126] The priority in the leadership of the local church is therefore in leadership through the ministers of the word. As one pastor explained, it is "the conviction that Christ rules the church and he rules by his Word and he appoints elders to guard that Word in the life of the church, to keep the church healthy ... you take care of the family by holding them to the Word of God—the word of Christ."

This principle creates a conflict if leadership is uncritically shared within the existing parochial structures: neither Churchwardens nor PCC members are required to be qualified for Word ministry, let alone be actively involved with it. Therefore in order for plural local leadership to be exercised by leaders involved in Word ministry, some kind of innovation will be required: either additional criteria are demanded of wardens and PCC so that they qualify as teachers who lead, or the Ministry Leadership Team is constituted in a different way to wardens and PCC.

The principle also speaks against a business model in which the PCC might be considered to be like a board of directors or governors. Under this model, the purpose of a board is to give oversight to the pastor who takes care of the shepherding ministry. But if board members are unqualified for the ministry of the word, how can they give oversight to those who are charged with it? Alternatively, board elders who are qualified to be elders but exercise no personal ministry are separating

---

[126] Calvin, John, *Institutes of the Christian Religion* (trans. Ford Lewis Battles, Philadelphia: The Westminster Press, 1965), IV.xiv.6. He is following Augustine *Against Faustus* xix.6.

what should be joined, namely the active shepherding ministry of the elders and the oversight ministry of governance. The first principle is therefore that pastoral leadership of the local church should be shared with teachers of the Word in the local church.

*Leaders Lead*

The incumbent is the senior pastor of the church, and also the leader of the elders, lay or ordained. Even where there is a clear commitment to the equal status of the fellow-MLT members, the pastor is expected to serve the church by leading the leaders too. Such leadership may mean taking the initiative when direction is needed, as one respondent explained: "I've begun to take the initiative and say 'What are we going to do? We need to do something.'" Or in the words of another, ensuring that spiritual priorities are maintained in the decision-making process, and "to be to some extent a guardian of sound teaching and doctrine." The MLT may challenge the overall leader as well as support him; they are to collaborate rather than merely co-operate. There is sufficient equality that any member of the MLT can and indeed should speak up. One pastor reflected on the resignation of an elder. "I have missed the robustness of the challenge to some of the things I wanted to say and do, which I think was healthy." And sometimes it is a challenge to find the balance between listening and leading. "You can't just say on everything, 'What do you think?' Sometimes I'll just say, 'This is the situation; my feeling is that I should do this, do you think that is a good idea?'" This is close to the point-leader position summed up by Gene Getz as "'I led the elders' and together 'we led the church.'"[127]

*Disciple-making Requires a Shepherding Ministry*

Each of the pastors interviewed leads a church in which personal ministry, or shepherding as defined in this study, plays a key role. To be sure, participants were at pains to emphasise that the ministry to the whole church, including the quality of preaching, is essential. But it is not sufficient. All were committed to a personal ministry that is the subject of this study. A MLT enables the senior pastor to remain engaged in personal ministry. "There's a danger I would have become several steps removed from the people, because I would have been busy doing all the big picture stuff. But sharing out the big picture stuff has meant I've been

---

[127] Getz, *Elders and Leaders*, p. 255.

able to ... stay more connected with people than I might have done. That I think has been one of the chief advantages."

Thus pastoral leadership is rightly shared with Word-ministers, and is concerned with individuals as well as with the big picture. It was notable that the range of concerns that called for pastoral attention was broader than merely reacting to the sick or the sinning. One participant's concern is to be "looking at the names of individuals, saying, 'What do they need? You know, are they in trouble? Do they need people to look after them, like physical, mental, emotional trouble? Are they in spiritual danger? Or are they people who actually, they've got gifts that need to be nurtured and deployed?'" Another's is "how can we encourage this person to take the next step in their discipleship and their growing as a Christian?"

*We are Normative Plus*

Historically Anglicans have been committed to the Normative Principle derived from the work of Richard Hooker.[128] The Anglican evangelical pastors in this study are best described as employing an informed Normative Plus hermeneutic, although not all would own the exact label. It means here that they are committed to a form of the Normative Principle in which Anglican structures are biblically informed and shaped, even as the structures are adapted to the specific context being served. It is thus Normative rather than Regulative, and the 'Plus' denotes the high emphasis on biblical patterns expressed in both structures and how the leaders within them behave.

*We are Confessionally Anglican*

All the pastors in the study identify as Anglican for that was one of the criteria for selecting participants. It was notable, however, that the further the church and minister were from being in a settled parish church within the Church of England, the more clearly they articulated their identity as Anglican, being both confessional and connectional — confessional in being rooted in the Formularies of the Church of England, sometimes with additional commitments such as Canon A5 or the Jerusalem Declaration, and connectional in expressing a desire to find some effective way to be in relationship with other churches and receiving

---

[128] See the discussion in Chapter Three.

oversight from outside the congregation.[129] The combination of Anglican self-identity and the Normative Plus hermeneutic led these churches to be conservative in changing the structures and yet creative about how to use those structures to bring about effective, biblically informed local ministry leadership.

*Biblically Informed Anglican Structures*

Churchwardens occupy an historical office, but in biblical categories their role is ambiguous. For some, wardens function as elders and any additional members of the MLT form "just a bigger group of wardens." For others the wardens are senior deacons and may act as a link between the MLT and the other councils of the church. The difference in role is significant in churches that are committed to male-only eldership as a consequence of complementarian theology (the view that men and women are equal before God and have different roles in leadership) because it determines whether or not it is appropriate for a woman to be a Churchwarden.

When a MLT emerges to share in the shepherding care of the church, the role of the PCC becomes more clearly defined as fulfilling diaconal roles. They are the 'doers' or in larger churches, the lead deacons. They are not tasked with the spiritual leadership of the church, whether it is agreeing preaching programs, or discussing the care of individuals let alone church discipline, or in initiating discussions of ministry strategy. Churches that established new congregations did not choose to create a new PCC but shared the practical tasks with teams. The council

---

[129] Canon A5 of the Church of England 'Of the doctrine of the Church of England' states that "the doctrine of the Church of England is grounded in the Holy Scriptures, and in such teachings of the ancient Fathers and Councils of the Church as are agreeable to the said Scriptures. In particular such doctrine is to be found in the Thirty-nine Articles of Religion, The Book of Common Prayer, and the Ordinal." The last three documents are the Formularies. The Jerusalem Declaration was issued by the Global Anglican Futures Conference (GAFCON) held in Jerusalem 22-29 June 2008. In the Declaration signatories join in "solemnly declaring the following tenets of orthodoxy which underpin our Anglican identity...." (http://fca.net/resources/the-complete-jerusalem-statement accessed 30 May 2016).

that unites the leaders of these teams would function in a similar way to the PCC.

A further thought on the PCC is that it may be considered as a representative of the church membership. The Church of England has only a fluid definition of membership because it is based on the Christendom model in which every resident of the parish has a claim on the church. The Electoral Roll consists of those who are willing to be associated with the church and entitles those found on the Roll to choose wardens and elect PCC members. All other decisions are taken by the PCC. Thus in comparison to a congregational system of church government, the PCC performs some of the functions of the members' meeting. That is also consistent with the qualifications for membership of the PCC gently reflecting the characteristics of a church member rather than those of a deacon or even elder.

The role of the staff is also ambiguous. Senior staff, that is, those whose role is public ministry and leadership and who are often ordained, function as elders; that much is straightforward. Staff members often have the time and expertise to follow up individuals, and mixed-sex staff teams allow for even coverage for men and women in the church. In the absence of a MLT, the normal place for shepherding discussions would be the staff team. A MLT is therefore needed if either (a) there is an ethical commitment to shared leadership with non-staff elders, or (b) there are insufficient staff. In all but one of the cases studied in this research, reason (a) dominated.

*The Role of Women*

The pastors in this study all identify as conservative evangelicals, and espouse a complementarian view of the Bible's teaching on the role of women in leadership within the local church. The following four statements may be made to summarise the pastors' understanding: (a) women are equal to men but have different roles; (b) elders should be male; (c) deacons may be men or women; and (d) nobody has worked out where the senior women fit in. "I don't really know that we've figured it out yet and that's...I'm on a journey there, nothing is sorted."

## Clear Benefits

The purpose of the study was to explore how ministers explain the benefits of a shared pastoral leadership team for the task of making disciples in contemporary Britain. And the benefits are clear. We may summarise them as follows:

*Resilience.* The pastor himself is better supported in sharing the personal stress of exercising pastoral responsibility when a MLT is in place to share the burden with him. Two respondents spoke openly about the health problems associated with having to lead alone, now mitigated by having a team in place.

*Coverage.* A plural structure enables greater coverage in the shepherding ministry because the lay elders are also engaged in the congregation. In a multi-congregation church, the pastor cannot be present at all sites on a given Sunday, but with a plural MLT, there is always somebody that a worshipper can go and talk to on a Sunday. A related advantage articulated by one pastor was accountability of the pastoral review team. For instance, having been tasked to follow up a person, "A week later we will say, have you followed them up?"

*Diversity/Wisdom.* The team's diversity brings additional gifts and wisdom to bear on pastoral care because "one size doesn't fit all." To be sure there are frustrations in working collaboratively because it may sometimes slow the leaders down and different personalities can also give rise to tensions.

*Diffusing Criticism.* A ministry leadership team can deflect criticism that would otherwise be borne by the pastor alone. One explained that he was able to meet congregational criticism with, "the [MLT] have considered this carefully," and give an appropriate explanation of the reasons. That helped the congregation understand the seriousness of sin. "I think it just sends out a different message," he added.

*Accountability of Leaders.* A leadership team may also make the pastor, and by implication the other leaders, more accountable to the congregation because their decisions are more visible. And conversely, having a ministry leadership team in place empowers the church members to ask their leaders for clarification or action.

*Healthy Biblical Practice.* Given the discussion above about being 'Normative Plus,' we do not expect Anglican pastors to cite as a benefit that plural eldership is 'biblical' because it is simply obedient to a biblical pattern *tout court.* However, a MLT reflects a biblically informed Anglican structure which allows for healthier patterns of church life. "I'm enjoying the environment of the [MLT], the church family understanding that there is a leadership team, I think it's much more healthy for the church." It was noted above in Chapter Two that for Hellerman plural leadership is biblical because the plurality approach offers a social context for Jesus-like exercise of authority.[130]

## Collaborative Working

Third, we can note that several practices enable and protect collaboration.

### I've Had to Change Shape Completely

Co-operation falls short of collaboration, as may be seen even in secular settings. Amy Edmondson, for example, defines collaboration as "a way of working with colleagues that is characterised by co-operation, mutual respect, and shared goals;"[131] Carole Orchard's study of collaborative working in healthcare identified power imbalances as one of the obstacles to collaboration.[132] Many more sources could be cited to make the point that simply telling people to collaborate will not enable them to do so.

The duties of the PCC are "co-operation with the incumbent in promoting in the parish the whole mission of the church, pastoral, evangelistic, social and ecumenical."[133] The wardens too are to "be foremost in representing the laity and in co-operating with the incumbent; they shall use their best endeavours by example and precept to encourage the parishioners in the practice of true religion and to promote unity and peace among them. They shall also maintain order and decency in the church and churchyard, especially during the time of

---

[130] Hellerman, *Embracing Shared Ministry*, pp. 169-170.
[131] Edmondson, Amy C., *Teaming: How Organizations Learn, Innovate, and Compete in the Knowledge Economy* (San Francisco: Jossey-Bass, 2012), p. 52.
[132] Carole A. Orchard, Gillian A.; King, Hossein Khalili, & Mary Beth Bezzina, 'Assessment of Interprofessional Team Collaboration Scale (AITCS): Development and Testing of the Instrument', *Journal of Continuing Education in the Health Professions*, 32/1 (2012): 58-67.
[133] The Parochial Church Councils (Powers) Measure 1956, s.2 as substituted by the Synodical Government Measure 1969, s.6. See also *Church Representation Rules* (2011 edn, London: Church House Publishing, 2011), pp. 15-25.

divine service."[134] Ministers used to gaining the co-operation of a PCC will need to learn new behaviours if they are genuinely to collaborate with members of a MLT. "I've had to understand that I'm working with others, rather than just having to convince a PCC or others that this is what we're going to do. I've had to change shape completely."

*Ethical Commitment*

The commitment to collaboration is an ethical commitment. The phrase is borrowed from Wilson and Cervero's study of education planning. When the different parties meet to plan educational provision, they are normally expected to deploy their own power to further their own interests; that is simply pragmatism. But if they make an ethical commitment to serve the interests of others, then they will strive to conduct the planning discussion in a way that enables those others' interests to be fairly represented.[135] In a similar way, pastors and MLTs' commitment to plurality and to collaboration in church is not mere pragmatism, although there are benefits that accrue to them. It is also an ethical commitment to work collaboratively for the health of the whole church and the health of their ministry in providing leadership. A consequence of the ethical commitment is that having decided to collaborate, the MLT members then need to agree how they will collaborate. In other words, they need to negotiate the collaboration space.

*Negotiating the Collaboration Space*

Discussions about how a group of people will conduct their business is termed a meta-negotiation, while the business itself is the substantive negotiation. Wilson and Cervero's study of working the planning table examines the meta-negotiation about who will be represented in the discussions. Siemens and others describe interdisciplinary research in which the nature of the collaboration itself "may range from relatively little task interdependence to a fully integrative process where researchers

---

[134] Canon E.1 'Of Churchwardens'. Their other responsibilities for allocation of seats and dispersal of alms have fallen into disuse. Briden, Timothy, & Kenneth M MacMorran, *A Handbook for Churchwardens and Parochial Church Councillors* (London: Mowbray, 1996), pp. 63-69.

[135] Arthur L. Wilson, & Ronald M. Cervero, 'Democracy and Program Planning', *New Directions for Adult & Continuing Education*, 128 (2010): 81-89.

work closely together on all aspects of the project."[136] Instead of searching for a 'right' or 'wrong' way to collaborate, Siemens *et al.* suggest a conceptual framework in which research teams can negotiate which point in the so-called collaboration space that they wish to occupy, as shown in Figure 1 Dimensions of the Collaboration Space. In a similar way, MLT members will need to discuss and agree how they will collaborate. For example one pastor shared, "There was some argy-bargy earlier on when someone said ... we should be having a say in the preaching programme and so on, and I'm thinking, 'Hang on a minute, I've always done this.' But we've worked that through." Staff elders also needed to agree with the non-staff lay elders how much detail was wanted. "What they do want to know, what they don't need to know, and what they want to—what sort of level they want to agree things on and what they want to get us to drill down and work out." Part of 'changing shape completely' is negotiating the collaboration space, which is about getting the right people together, to work in the right way.

In a similar way, the ethical commitment to shared leadership in a church impacts the composition to ensure that those who should lead are present. Another outcome of a meta-negotiation might therefore be deliberately to include non-elders so that their interests are represented. This conclusion might lead to the inclusion of female pastoral leaders, or non-elder wardens, or staff such as an administrator. Liaison with other bodies in the church as PCC or trustees will also need to be borne in mind, even if they are not formally represented.

---

[136] Lynne Siemens, Liu Yin, & Jefferson Smith, 'Mapping Disciplinary Differences and Equity of Academic Control to Create a Space for Collaboration', *Canadian Journal of Higher Education*, 44/2 (2014), p. 50.

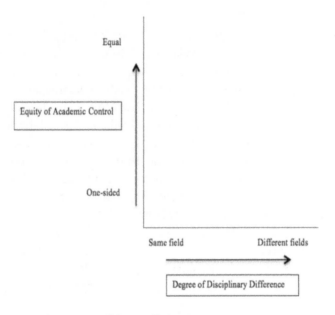

**Figure 1: Dimensions of the Collaboration Space**

*Who knows Eric?*

Because of the importance of personal ministry, the 'right people' must include those who are engaged in discipleship, that is (micro-) shepherding. Even in those MLTs that are not able to spend much time on individuals, perhaps because of the size of the church, disciple-making is still a criterion for potential lay elders. In Strauch's terms, they are to be shepherd elders rather than business-like "board elders."[137]

When the MLT consists of those engaged in shepherding ministry, there can be collaborative pastoral leadership. If 'Eric' comes to pastoral notice and the benefits of plural pastoral leadership include coverage and diversity, then the discussion can begin with the question, "Who knows Eric?" to reveal which of the persons present are already engaged with that person. Indeed one of the challenges of shared pastoring is communication. As one respondent put it, "You can sometimes end up with a situation where you can suddenly leap in to support somebody only to discover that somebody else has been visiting them twice a week for the last three months." When the right people are

---

[137] Strauch, *Biblical Eldership*, p. 31. See also above in Chapter Three.

gathered into a MLT, then the question "Who knows Eric" will find an answer.

The 'Who knows Eric' test also explains why the so-called College of Presbyters around a bishop, or indeed a local deanery clergy chapter, cannot effectively share pastoral concern. Unless the presbyters are serving an area so small that they do in fact 'know Eric', they cannot meaningfully collaborate and achieve the plural local leadership patterned on the New Testament churches. Therefore neither a College nor a deanery can be effective in sharing pastoral oversight.

*Methodological Levelling*

One of the clearest imbalances on a MLT is between staff and non-staff members because the former usually have more time, training, and capacity to bring to bear on ministry issues than their non-staff counterparts. This kind of situation is not unique to ministry. In education, for example, students and faculty can collaborate as learning communities to facilitate learning, but students are understandably anxious about taking part in public discussions with faculty whose knowledge and power far exceed their own. DeLathouwer and others studied the role of workshops designed to mitigate the perceived imbalance. This deliberate strategy to overcome structural barriers to collaboration was named methodological levelling.[138] In a similar way, pastors and MLTs can employ deliberate strategies to mitigate the imbalance in capacity between staff and non-staff MLT members and the following were noted in the findings: all the pastors circulate documents for discussion in advance of the meetings. Other strategies include taking time over decisions, putting MLT members through a Strengths Finder analysis,[139] and also seeing in every discussion an opportunity for training through the pastor sharing his thinking. Imbalances in capacity and training do exist between members, and these may well impede good collaboration. These imbalances can be addressed by negotiating the collaboration space — that is, agreeing how the MLT wants to work —

---

[138] Erin DeLathouwer, Wendy Roy, Ann Martin, & Jasmine Liska, 'Multidisciplinary Collaboration Through Learning Communities: Navigating Anxiety', *Collected Essays on Learning and Teaching V* (Hamilton, ON: Society for Teaching and Learning in Higher Education, 2012), p. 28.

[139] Rath, Tom, *Strengths Finder 2.0* (New York: Gallup Press, 2007).

and by methodological levelling or using deliberate strategies to change the dynamic.

*Leadership is an Us*

The final practice that enables collaborative working is the deliberate presentation of the MLT as a team. In other words the incumbent learns to move from 'I have decided' through 'The MLT and I have decided' to 'The MLT have decided.' One pastor explained how when a change was introduced in church in this way, "When the criticism came, it wasn't a huge amount, but the flak came [n] ways rather than one way, and that was just immensely helpful."[140] In another situation, when the approach to a difficult pastoral situation requiring church discipline had been agreed by the MLT rather than by himself acting alone, the pastor could know that he "was going as a representative, if you like, of the church family, bringing God's Word to bear on [the person concerned] from the church family, rather than some sort of dictator."

## Conclusion

We have seen from the foregoing that locally shared pastoral leadership in a Ministry Leadership Team is beneficial both for the church and for the leaders themselves. This chapter summarised the experiences of pastors holding to common commitments yet having found different implementations of the principle of plural leadership. Instead of seeking a structural single solution, we need instead to explore the contours of the existing structures and explore the options for locating a MLT in the midst of them. These options are outlined in the next chapter.

---

[140] Where [n] is the number of leaders on that church's MLT.

## 5. Practical Proposals

We have seen how the solo pastorate became established as the normal pattern for ministry within Christendom as a result of historical development. As a consequence of the new challenges of ministry in post-Christendom, as well as the greater desire for biblically informed structures and practice, the case for locally shared pastoral leadership is being made more urgently than before. And the benefits, as far as those interviewed are concerned, are clear. There remains the practical task of accommodating a Ministry Leadership Team within the existing legal structures of the local parish church. The options are either that one colonises the other, that the two are in conflict, or that some innovative thinking is required. The main options are surveyed below. It will be remembered from the previous chapter that no single 'best' solution had emerged from the sample of churches examined.

A structure alone is not sufficient to enable collaborative leadership: we saw in Chapter Four that key principles need to be in place as well as practices that promote good collaboration. Shared leadership, then, is not only about who meets together, but also about how they meet. In that way it can become the kind of social context in which, with Hellerman, we can look for the Jesus-like exercise of authority.

### Lay Offices in the Church of England

The office of Churchwarden is an ancient one. As we saw in Chapter Four, they are the senior lay leaders responsible both to the congregation and to the bishop and their formal responsibilities are to "be foremost in representing the laity and in co-operating with the incumbent."[141] It may be noted that they are not required to teach or administer discipline, although their 'endeavours by … precept' might have a bearing on the spiritual health of the congregation. Nor are Churchwardens subject to the criteria for eldership laid out in 1 Timothy 3:1-7 and Titus 1:6-9. They are required only to be sixteen years of age or more, be actual communicants, and willing to serve.[142]

---

[141] Canon E.1 'Of Churchwardens', cited above Chapter Four 'Collaborative Working'.
[142] Church of England, *Church Representation Rules*, pp. 11, 63. This is a minimum, of course.

The Parochial Church Council (PCC) is the decision-making body of the church and it makes financial and legal decisions on behalf of the church. It is responsible for drawing up a budget, administering the church's financial and other assets, and regulating the employment of staff and clerks (but not the incumbent).[143] The incumbent may only change the time and form of services in consultation with the PCC, and appointments of leaders working with children and vulnerable adults must be approved by the PCC for insurance purposes. However the PCC does not have formal responsibility for the ministry of the Word, nor for discipline, nor indeed for recruitment and deployment of other volunteers. The members of the PCC are elected for three years and unlike Churchwardens, are not required to be actual communicants.[144]

Readers, self-supporting ministers, and others licensed for ministry have no formal responsibility to share in decision-making within the church.[145] In order to progress a nomination for someone to be admitted as a Reader, the bishop must be satisfied that the person is "of good life, sound in faith, a regular communicant, and well fitted for the work of a Reader."[146] There is no expectation that Readers share in leadership (beyond their PCC membership), and in the case of a vacancy in the parish, responsibility for the parish devolves to the rural dean and the Churchwardens, and not to the Readers or self-supporting ministers.

None of the above roles constitute a collaborative local eldership: Churchwardens and PCC are not required to meet the same standards as Readers, let alone ordained presbyters. The lay officers are required only to 'co-operate' with the incumbent, which falls short of collaboration. Where collaboration is mandated between the incumbent, Churchwardens, and PCC, it covers governance, fabric, and finance, rather than pastoral matters. Equally, while the incumbent, Readers, and any self-supporting ministers may choose to exercise a collaborative ministry, it does not imply that decision making and responsibility are necessarily shared between them.

---

[143] Briden, Timothy, & Brian Hanson, *Moore's Introduction to English Canon Law.* (3rd edn, London: Mowbray, 1992), p. 35.
[144] Church of England, *Church Representation Rules*, pp. 55-56.
[145] Readers are *ex-officio* members of the PCC. Church of England, *Church Representation Rules*, p. 15.
[146] Canon E.5 'Of the nomination and admission of Readers', para. 2.

There is therefore no established structure for the work of presbyter or elder to be shared locally between the incumbent and others within the local church. As one minister put it, a weakness of Anglican polity is that "legally the buck stops with the vicar, the rector, whatever. And that is legally the situation."

## Possible ways to accommodate a MLT

The responsibility that needs to be shared for plural local pastoral leadership is conveyed in the phrase "the cure of souls." In his survey of pastoral ministry, Vanhoozer explains that "Pastor-theologians tend to the flock and cultivate God's field when they oversee or (to use the traditional term) 'cure' souls. The cure of souls means caring for a person's deepest self: the orientation of the heart towards other persons and especially towards God." [147] Legally in the Church of England this rests with the incumbent and is otherwise shared only with the bishop. When a new incumbent is instituted to a post, the bishop presents the deed of institution with the words "Receive this cure of souls, which is both yours and mine."

The care of property and assets, on the other hand, is in the hands of the Churchwardens and PCC. There is therefore a distinction between the ministry of shepherding the sheep (the cure of souls) and the ministry of management of assets (the care of stuff).

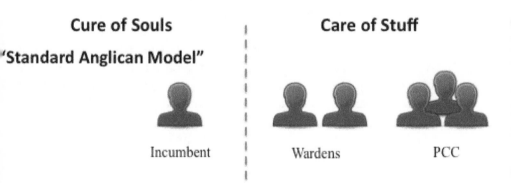

## Cure of Souls      Care of Stuff
### "Standard Anglican Model"

Incumbent      Wardens      PCC

**Figure 2: The Cure of Souls and the Care of Stuff**

---

[147] Vanhoozer, & Strachan, *Pastor as Public Theologian*, pp. 144-145.

Any arrangement for plural local oversight involves the sharing of the incumbent's ministry without taking away any of the PCC's responsibilities. It is also clear that because there is no existing format for locally shared pastoral oversight, some kind of innovation will be needed. Several different solutions are briefly examined below.

*Incumbent and Wardens as a Plural Eldership*

Under this model, the wardens are lay elders and are recognised before the church as working in a leadership team. The wardens are naturally seen as senior lay people, but usually each church has only two wardens who also have other legal duties to fulfil. While the office of Churchwarden is not found in Scripture, its practice can be informed by biblical categories. We noted above (Chapter Four, 'Biblically Informed Anglican Structures') that the role of Churchwarden is ambiguous and they may be considered to be either elders or senior deacons. If they are treated as elders, then the Incumbent and Wardens form a Ministry Leadership Team.

There is much to commend the model of the incumbent and Churchwardens acting as the church's plural eldership: they are the senior ordained and lay members of the church respectively, all are *ex-officio* members of the PCC and as a group they are entirely congruent with the church's legal structures. The weaknesses are that because Churchwardens are not required by canon law to meet the criteria for eldership, they cannot be removed for falling short of those criteria. It is up to the incumbent and the PCC to ensure that only suitable candidates are elected as Churchwardens, and the ability to work this model depends heavily on the incumbent's personal political power. This may reduce the wardens' ability to act as check and balance on the incumbent's power. A second weakness is that this group is small. If senior staff such as an Associate Minister, and other senior lay leaders are added to the group, the automatic congruence with PCC may be lost unless the additional members are also members of the PCC.

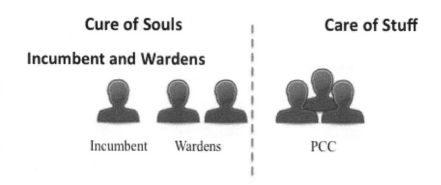

**Figure 3: Incumbent and Wardens as Eldership**

*Standing Committee as a Plural Eldership*

In this model the Standing Committee of the PCC acts as the plural leadership of the church. Once again, membership is coherent with the existing structures because the incumbent and Churchwardens are members *ex officio*, and the Standing Committee has powers to act by delegation from the full PCC. As a body larger than just incumbent and wardens, it may now include some staff members and other ministry leaders from the congregation. It is not necessary to include the PCC Secretary and Treasurer in the Standing Committee although this may commonly be the case.[148] The weakness is that such a body may only be informally constituted, and there is no legal means to exclude members who are fit for PCC membership but unsuited to the exercise of pastoral leadership. Once again, this model depends on the ability of the whole PCC to elect a standing committee competent to provide Collaborative Leadership to the church.

---

[148] Church of England, *Church Representation Rules*, pp. 80-81.

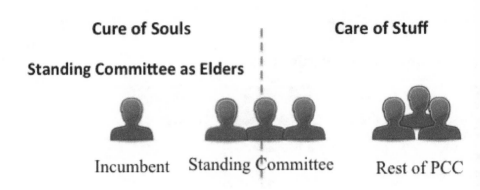

**Figure 4: Standing Committee as Eldership**

*PCC as a Plural Eldership*

A PCC is not a small body. Depending on the size of the church, there are between six and fifteen elected members, not counting *ex-officio* members. The PCC is not formally charged with responsibility for the spiritual ministry of the church, and this is reflected in the low standard required for election to the PCC noted above. It is a right instinct for the incumbent to want to share his ministry, but the PCC is the wrong body with whom to seek to share it. The incumbent and the PCC have different responsibilities and if the PCC shares the incumbent's pastoral responsibilities, some other body may need to be found to discharge the PCC's own duties for the 'care of stuff'.

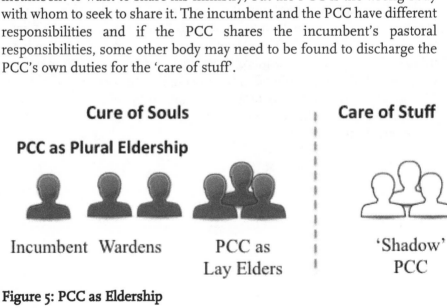

**Figure 5: PCC as Eldership**

In terms of biblically informed categories, the PCC is not an expanded eldership. It may be either considered to be a gathering of deacons, or in larger churches, lead deacons. Or it may be considered as a representative membership, which is at least consistent with the generous criteria for election.

*Staff Team as a Plural Eldership*

This pattern is attractive for practical reasons. Paid staff have the time, capacity, and usually training for providing pastoral care. If they report to the incumbent, their work can be efficiently coordinated. And further, where they are engaged in the public ministry of the Word through teaching and leading worship, they become the natural points of contact for those seeking pastoral counsel. However the pastors in this study are looking for more than a merely practical solution. They seek biblically informed practice, and their reading of the Bible's teaching prompts them to an ethical commitment to seek a plural eldership that deliberately includes non-staff lay elders —even if it makes life more difficult. Indeed in one church investigated in this project, the staff explicitly have no formal role in the church's leadership structure, while in another they play a large part in overseeing pastoral care but in a framework that also includes non-staff lay elders. For principled reasons, therefore, the staff should not be the only elders. Staff teams can provide effective pastoral care, and in particular can provide a good way for female pastoral leaders to be involved without undermining the principle of male-only eldership.

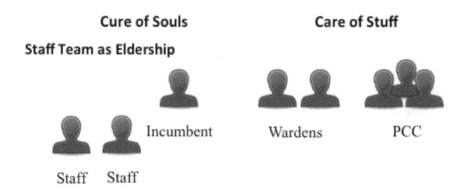

**Cure of Souls**        **Care of Stuff**

**Staff Team as Eldership**

Incumbent      Wardens      PCC

Staff   Staff

**Figure 6: Staff Team as Eldership**

## *Home Group Leaders and Service Leaders as a Plural Eldership*

The small groups form the front line of pastoral care within a local church and their leaders are therefore very much involved in pastoral care within the church. The issue here is about how that pastoral care should be overseen and directed. The churches in our study had both small group leaders and a MLT, and in several cases the MLT members were also small group leaders.

Service leaders also provide visible leadership. In a multi-congregation church, the pastor cannot be present at all sites on a given Sunday, but with a plural MLT, there can always be somebody available for worshippers on any given Sunday. Service leaders might therefore be a natural choice as MLT members because of their visible and public ministry. In one multi-site church, each congregation had its own MLT whose duties included public leadership of that congregation so that congregation members have a visible leader.

A MLT could therefore be constituted of those who exercise leadership in small groups and service leadership. A possible weakness of this approach is that the organisation may be more hierarchical than collaborative. With small groups, for instance, primary pastoral care is given in groups, with more difficult cases referred upward to the minister. In a larger church, the small groups may be organised into clusters with a coordinator but the same hierarchical principle of delegation remains.

Small group leaders and service leaders may be the kind of people who should be part of a MLT; nevertheless, a MLT is an additional, explicit group that exists for more than the coordination of small groups or of service leading. The leaders of small groups and the service leaders need not form a MLT by virtue of their roles; rather their roles identify them as people who would be suitable for MLT if they have the additional capacity to serve in this way.

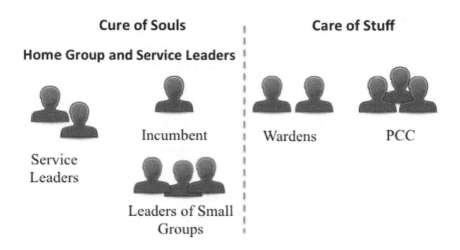

**Figure 7: Home Group Leaders and Service Leaders**

*"College of Presbyters" as a Plural Eldership under the Bishop*

This option may be attractive for historical reasons because it seems to promise a return to the situation that existed before the conversion of the Roman Empire. We saw earlier how the expansion of the churches led to the isolation of the presbyters. [149] The notion that a College of Presbyters can be a plural eldership appears to offer a return to an early church model.

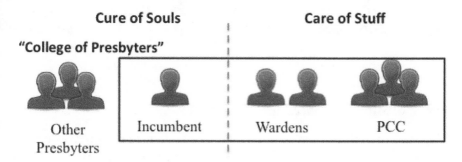

**Figure 8: "College of Presbyters"**

---

[149] See above Chapter Three, "History and the shape of ministry up to the Reformation".

The model cannot be commended, however, on the grounds of both principle and practicality outlined in previous chapters. On principle, the local unit of the visible church is the local church not the deanery or diocese; and as a matter of practicality, the college of presbyters or deanery chapter fails the "Who knows Eric?" test. Claiming a shared oversight with presbyters in other churches is not a solution because it does nothing to enhance the pastoral care of individuals in the local church.

*Ministry Leadership Team as a Plural Eldership*

A Ministry Leadership Team is a group of suitably qualified persons who are recognised by the church as those who share shepherding leadership with the incumbent. The MLT is identified as the team giving *leadership* in the area of *ministry*, which is not formally the PCC's remit. As a *team*, the MLT is expected to work collaboratively. It may therefore contain both paid and volunteer ministry leaders. Their role is to share both its macro- and micro- dimensions, to use Witmer's terminology. The MLT shares the work of the incumbent ('Cure of souls') without taking away that of the PCC ('Care of stuff').

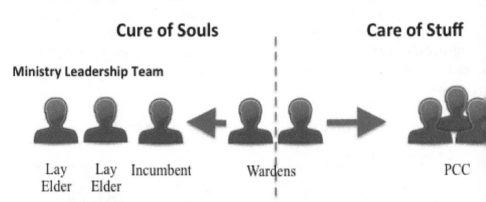

**Figure 9: Ministry Leadership Team (MLT)**

The MLT therefore consists of those qualified to give spiritual oversight. As we saw in the key principle of letting teachers lead, the MLT consists of those qualified as elders in this way. Their role is to act collaboratively, under the leadership of the pastor, to care spiritually for the flock. Rather than inhabit one of the existing structures, such as standing committee or PCC, the MLT is identified as a new body that works with the pastor. The closest overlap is with the incumbent and wardens group.

The key element is the relationship of this team to the PCC and other formal structures. As a leadership structure, the MLT needs authority to make decisions and see them through, and as decision-making authority is vested in the PCC, there must be overlap between the MLT and PCC if conflict is to be avoided. David Watson's model was to choose a MLT such that most members were also on the PCC, so that PCC could with confidence support MLT decisions and still retain an element of accountability. He explains:

> a strong representation [by elders on the PCC] would seem important to avoid any possibility of tension between the two groups. However since the PCC must inevitably deal with more administrative and financial matters, and since the elders attend more to the pastoral and disciplinary aspects of the work, it is unlikely that all elders will be, or need to be, on the PCC.[150]

In this sense it is an extension of the Incumbent and Wardens model:

> In some churches it might be right for the Churchwardens or the Standing Committee to form the first eldership. What is important is that the elders should be marked for their *spiritual* maturity and not necessarily for their official position in the church.[151]

Watson's elders were nominated by him and compared with the church's nominations. "The church is not a democracy, and the elders have always been ultimately my appointment, although checked by the congregation in the way described."[152] Since Watson wrote, the greater emphasis on accountability of ordained leaders and the benefit of non-staff elders mean that were he writing today, Watson might well express himself differently. Within the churches surveyed there was invariably a mechanism by which a potential MLT member was proposed to the congregation, which is asked to ratify the appointment.

A MLT becomes more important when the key principles are strongly upheld in the church's ministry. These principles state that

---

[150] Watson, *I Believe in the Church*, p. 295.
[151] Watson, *I Believe in the Church*, p. 295.
[152] Watson, *I Believe in the Church*, p. 292.

teachers of the Word should lead, rather than administrators and deacons of the PCC; that shepherding must be an essential component of both ministry and leadership; that it should be shared and not rest on the incumbent's shoulders alone; and that existing structures can be biblically informed and adapted accordingly.

A consequence of the adoption of a MLT is clarity on the role of the PCC. It is not an eldership, and becomes more of a diaconate tasked with providing practical support to the church's spiritual leadership.

## Issues to Consider

Three comments may be made about the relationship between the MLT and PCC. The first is to ensure good communication between the two bodies. Usually the incumbent and one or two others will be members of both groups. That overlap provides liaison and communication, without confusing the remits of the two groups. In one church, for instance, the PCC has a standing item to hear what is being discussed at Ministry Leadership Team, and invited to pray, but the discussion and the decision remain the MLT's if it affects pastoral practice and priorities.

The second issue is clarity as to which matters are discussed by which group. One pastor described his role as deciding which body should discuss a certain question. "I'm thinking where does this need to go, is this a [MLT] thing? Is this a staff team thing? Is this a something else thing?" At face value that model assumes that the discussion needs to take place either in one setting or in another, be it MLT, staff, or PCC. In practice a ministry issue may have implications for several areas of church life. For example the decision to plant a new congregation is taken first for missional and spiritual reasons; yet it has potentially massive practical implications. Is it a MLT thing or a PCC thing? RACI analysis, for example, allows that different bodies have different levels of involvement according to whether they are responsible (R) for carrying out the task, accountable (A) for its execution, required to be consulted (C), or have a right to be informed (I).[153] In a similar way, it may be that that a key decision in church life is who has the authority to initiate a

---

[153] See for example Thomas Frauman, 'Improving the effectiveness of strategy implementation through use of RACI charts', *Asia Pacific Coatings Journal*, 25/5 (2012): 39-40; Thomas Frauman, 'Using RACI charts to drive more powerful execution of business strategy', *Asia Pacific Coatings Journal*, 25/6 (2012): 25-27.

discussion and how it progresses from there. For instance the MLT can propose planting a new congregation and once the idea has reached a certain stage, it might be handed on to the PCC to elaborate some of the practical details. Similarly the MLT may decide for ministry reasons on a change of format to the Sunday services, and the PCC then be consulted and asked to agree. But the PCC would not be expected to take the first lead in either of those cases. The division of labour between MLT and PCC is therefore not only a question of who discusses a particular issue but may be a matter of who discusses it *first* and who signs off on it *last*. Author and surgeon Atul Gawande describes a problem-solving process in the construction industry which may be pertinent. If a situation arises on-site with respect to, say, the steel frame of a building, then a checklist details which other contractors must be consulted and must each sign off on the proposed solution before it can be implemented.[154] These and other works might provide a creative grid to guide the interaction between MLT, PCC and any other bodies such as Trustees.

The third area to consider is whether deliberate overlap between MLT and other bodies can enable the participation of women in churches that hold to male-only eldership. The meetings of the MLT, especially those concerned for the care of individuals, may include additional members such as a female pastoral worker or an administrator who is also female and who facilitates the meeting. As has been admitted in the interviews, such additions are an accommodation to the desire to include women, even though the most theologically coherent way to do so remains unclear at present.

## Conclusion

The option that is most attractive will depend on the context, with the key factor being the Churchwardens. If they are to function as elders, then the MLT is essentially an Incumbent and Wardens group, to which other suitable individuals may be added. But there may be good reasons why the wardens do not function as elders, such as the difficulty of delegating the diaconal duties that come with the role, or the desire to retain someone who is excellently suited to the role of senior deacon. In that case the appointment of a MLT allows suitably qualified elder-types to

---

[154] Gawande, Atul, *The Checklist Manifesto: How to Get Things Right* (New York: Metropolitan Books, 2010).

share the incumbent's shepherding ministry, with support from the wardens in their ministry. In a church with larger staff, the MLT may more closely resemble a senior staff meeting with lay elders in addition. Again it is a matter of context whether the lay elders are wardens or not.

## Summary

Thus study has examined the case for plural local pastoral leadership from the biblical, historical and pastoral data. The case for locally shared pastoral leadership among Anglicans is that it represents the social context for a biblically-informed exercise of leadership in the local church. Such an understanding is in line with the Normative Principle, and shows benefits in the health of the local church and its leaders. No single pattern for implementation was found among the churches surveyed, confirming the importance of context in determining the shape of ministry, even where common principles are clearly shared. However locally shared pastoral leadership is put into practice, it revolves around gathering the right people, that is those qualified for pastoral leadership, in the right way, that is for collaboration, and for the right purposes, that is to further the shepherding ministry of the church.

## Acknowledgements

I would first and foremost like to thank my wife Christa who patiently supported me during the research and writing, and to Wembdon PCC for support and time with the underlying research. A special mention goes to Bob & Maureen Ballard whose hospitality gave me physical and emotional space to read and write.

The pastors who took part in the study must remain nameless: nevertheless I am grateful to them for their time and attention, and for the encouragement they provided to me even during the process of hearing their experience and wisdom. I thank God for these men and their evident love for his people.

# Bibliography of Items Cited

Adams, Edward, *The Earliest Christian Meeting Places: Almost Exclusively Houses?* (London: Bloomsbury T & T Clark, 2013).

Atkinson, David, 'Evangelicalism and Pastoral Ministry', in R T France, and Alister McGrath (eds), *Evangelical Anglicans: Their Role and Influence in the Church Today* (London: SPCK, 1993): pp. 147-159.

Barrett, C. K., *Church, Ministry and Sacraments in the New Testament* (Exeter: Paternoster, 1985).

Baxter, Richard, *The Reformed Pastor* (Edinburgh: Banner of Truth Trust, 1974).

Beckwith, Roger, *Elders in Every City: The Origin and Role of the Ordained Ministry* (Carlisle: Paternoster Press, 2003).

Bradshaw, Paul F., *The Anglican Ordinal: Its History and Development From the Reformation to the Present Day* (London: SPCK for the Alcuin Club, 1971).

Bradshaw, Timothy, *The Olive Branch: An Evangelical Anglican Doctrine of the Church* (Carlisle: Paternoster Press for Latimer House, 1992).

Bray, Gerald L., *The Faith We Confess: An Exposition of the Thirty-Nine Articles* (London: The Latimer Trust, 2009).

Bray, Gerald L., 'The Pastor as Evangelical and Anglican', in Melvin Tinker (ed.), *The Renewed Pastor: Essays on the Pastoral Ministry in Honour of Philip Hacking* (Fearn: Christian Focus, 2011): pp. 239-255.

Bray, Gerald L., 'Why I Am an Evangelical and an Anglican', in Anthony L Chute, Christopher W Morgan, and Robert A Peterson (eds), *Why We Belong* (Wheaton, IL: Crossway, 2013): pp. 65-92.

Briden, Timothy, and Brian Hanson, *Moore's Introduction to English Canon Law.* (3rd edn, London: Mowbray, 1992).

Briden, Timothy, and Kenneth M MacMorran, *A Handbook for Churchwardens and Parochial Church Councillors* (London: Mowbray, 1996).

Brierley, Peter, 'Churchmanship of Churches 1989-2005', *U K Christian Handbook,* 6 (2006): Table 5.14.

Brierley, Peter, 'Geography, Christians and Those With No Religion', *Future First,* 34 (2014): 2, accessed October 7, 2015, http://www.brierleyconsultancy.com/s/510217_FUTURE_FIRST_Issue-34.

Brierley, Peter, 'UK Religion', *Future First,* 30 (2013): 2-3 accessed October 7, 2016, http://www.brierleyconsultancy.com/s/ff30.pdf.

Brierley, Peter, 'Church Attendance', *Future First,* 33 (2014): 2, accessed October 10, 2016, http://www.brierleyconsultancy.com/s/508632_FUTURE_FIRST_Issue-33.

Brown, Raymond E., *The Epistles of John* (Garden City, NY: Doubleday, 1982).

Bruce, F. F., *The Epistles of John* (London: Pickering & Inglis, 1970).

Calvin, John, *Institutes of the Christian Religion* (trans. Ford Lewis Battles, Philadelphia: The Westminster Press, 1965).

Carson, D. A., Mark Ashton, R. Kent Hughes, and Timothy Keller, *Worship By the Book* (Grand Rapids, MI: Zondervan, 2002).

Chapple, Allan, 'Getting Romans to the Right Romans: Phoebe and the Delivery of St Paul's Letter', *Tyndale Bulletin,* 62/2 (2011): 195-214.

Church of England, *Mission-Shaped Church: Church Planting and Fresh Expressions of Church in a Changing Context* (London: Church House Publishing, 2004).

Church of England, *Church Representation Rules* (2011 edn, London: Church House Publishing, 2011).

Paul E Engle, and Steve B Cowan (eds), *Who Runs the Church? Four Views on Church Government* (Grand Rapids, MI: Zondervan, 2004).

Dawswell, Andrew, *Ministry Leadership Teams: Theory and Practice in Effective Collaborative Ministry* (Cambridge: Grove Books, 2003).

DeLathouwer, Erin, Wendy Roy, Ann Martin, and Jasmine Liska, 'Multidisciplinary Collaboration Through Learning Communities: Navigating Anxiety', *Collected Essays on Learning and Teaching V* (Hamilton, ON: Society for Teaching and Learning in Higher Education, 2012): pp. 27-32.

Dever, Mark, and Paul Alexander, *The Deliberate Church* (Wheaton, IL: Crossway, 2005).

Dulles, Avery, *Models of the Church* (Dublin: Gill and Macmillan, 1974).

Echlin, Edward P., *The Story of Anglican Ministry* (Slough: St Paul Publications, 1974).

Edmondson, Amy C., *Teaming: How Organizations Learn, Innovate, and Compete in the Knowledge Economy* (San Francisco: Jossey-Bass, 2012).

Francis, Leslie J, Susan H Jones, and Mandy Robbins, 'Clergy Personality and Collaborative Ministry: The Way Ahead for Stable Extraverts?', *Pastoral Psychology*, 53/1 (2004): 33-42.

Frauman, Thomas, 'Improving the effectiveness of strategy implementation through use of RACI charts', *Asia Pacific Coatings Journal*, 25/5 (2012): 39-40.

Frauman, Thomas, 'Using RACI charts to drive more powerful execution of business strategy', *Asia Pacific Coatings Journal*, 25/6 (2012): 25-27.

Gawande, Atul, *The Checklist Manifesto: How to Get Things Right* (New York: Metropolitan Books, 2010).

George, Timothy F., 'Why I Am an Evangelical and a Baptist', in Anthony L Chute, Christopher W Morgan, and Robert A Peterson (eds), *Why We Belong* (Wheaton. IL: Crossway, 2013): pp. 93-110.

Getz, Gene A., *Elders and Leaders: God's Plan for Leading the Church: A Biblical, Historical, and Cultural Perspective* (Chicago: Moody Publishers, 2003).

Green, Michael, *Freed to Serve: Training and Equipping for Ministry* (2nd edn, London: Hodder and Stoughton, 1988).

Greenwood, Robin, *The Ministry Team Handbook* (London: SPCK, 2000).

Hellerman, Joseph, *Embracing Shared Ministry: Power and Status in the Early Church and Why it Matters Today* (Grand Rapids, MI: Kregel, 2013).

Holloway, David, 'What is an Anglican Evangelical?', in Melvin Tinker (ed.), *Restoring the Vision: Anglican Evangelicals Speak Out* (Crowborough: MARC, 1990): pp. 15-38.

Jobes, Karen H., *1, 2, and 3 John* (Grand Rapids, MI: Zondervan, 2014).

Lane, William L., *Hebrews 9-12* (Dallas: Word Books, 1991).

Laniak, Timothy S, *Shepherds After My Own Heart: Pastoral Traditions and Leadership in the Bible* (Leicester: Apollos, 2006).

Lightfoot, Joseph Barber, 'Excursus: The Synonymes 'Bishop' and 'Presbyter'', *Saint Paul's Epistle to the Philippians: A Revised Text With Introduction, Notes, and Dissertations* (12th edn, London: Macmillan, 1898): pp. 95-99.

Lightfoot, Joseph Barber, 'The Christian Ministry', *Saint Paul's Epistle to the Philippians: A Revised Text With Introduction, Notes, and Dissertations* (12th edn, London: Macmillan, 1898): pp. 181-269.

Malphurs, Aubrey, *Advanced Strategic Planning: A 21st Century Model for Church and Ministry Leaders* (3rd edn, Grand Rapids, MI: Baker Books, 2013).

McGrath, Alister, 'Evangelical Anglicans: A Contradiction in Terms?', in R T France, and Alister McGrath (eds), *Evangelical Anglicans: Their Role and Influence in the Church Today* (London: SPCK, 1993): pp. 10-21.

Moll, C D E, 'Anglican Elders? Shared Pastoral Leadership in Anglican Churches', D. Min. Covenant Theological Seminary, St Louis, MO (2017).

Moo, Douglas J., *The Epistle to the Romans* (Grand Rapids, MI: Wm. B. Eerdmans, 1996).

Motyer, Alec, 'The Meaning of Ministry', in Melvin Tinker (ed.), *Restoring the Vision: Anglican Evangelicals Speak Out*

(Crowborough: MARC, 1990): pp. 229-254.

Motyer, Alec, *The Message of James: The Tests of Faith* (Leicester: Inter-Varsity Press, 2000).

Murray, Stuart, *Post-Christendom: Church and Mission in a Strange New World* (Carlisle: Paternoster, 2004).

Orchard, Carole A., Gillian A.; King, Hossein Khalili, and Mary Beth Bezzina, 'Assessment of Interprofessional Team Collaboration Scale (AITCS): Development and Testing of the Instrument', *Journal of Continuing Education in the Health Professions*, 32/1 (2012): 58-67.

Packer, J I, and N T Wright, *Anglican Evangelical Identity: Yesterday and Today* (London: Latimer Trust, 2008).

Rath, Tom, *Strengths Finder 2.0* (New York: Gallup Press, 2007).

Rayburn, Robert S., 'Ministers, Elders, and Deacons', in Mark R. Brown (ed.), *Order in the Offices: Essays Defining the Roles of Church Officers* (Duncansville, PA: Classic Presbyterian Government Resources, 1993): pp. 223-227.

Ryken, Philip Graham, *City on a Hill: Reclaiming the Biblical Pattern for the Church in the 21st Century* (Chicago: Moody Publishers, 2003).

Sceats, David, 'Gildas Savianas Redivivus - the Reformed Pastor, Richard Baxter', *Anvil*, 10/2 (1993): 135-145.

Schreiner, Thomas R., *Romans* (Grand Rapids, MI: Baker Academic, 1998).

Siemens, Lynne, Liu Yin, and Jefferson Smith, 'Mapping Disciplinary Differences and Equity of Academic Control to Create a Space for Collaboration', *Canadian Journal of Higher Education*, 44/2 (2014): 49-67.

Smalley, Stephen S., *1, 2, 3 John* (Revised edn, Nashville: Thomas Nelson, 2009).

Stott, John R. W., *The Contemporary Christian* (Leicester: IVP, 1992).

Stott, John R. W., *The Living Church: The Convictions of a Lifelong*

*Pastor* (Nottingham: Inter-Varsity Press, 2007).

Strauch, Alexander, *Biblical Eldership: An Urgent Call to Restore Biblical Church Leadership* (Revised and expanded edn, Littleton, CO: Lewis and Roth Publishers, 1995).

Summers, Gillian, 'Evangelicals and Patterns of Ministry', in R T France, and Alister McGrath (eds), *Evangelical Anglicans: Their Role and Influence in the Church Today* (London: SPCK, 1993): pp. 160-173.

Timmis, Steve, and Tim Chester, *Everyday Church: Mission By Being Good Neighbours* (Nottingham: IVP, 2011).

Turnbull, Richard, *Anglican and Evangelical?* (London: Continuum, 2007).

Vanhoozer, Kevin J., *Biblical Authority After Babel: Retrieving the Solas in the Spirit of Mere Protestant Christianity* (Kindle edn, Grand Rapics, MI: Brazos Press, 2016).

Vanhoozer, Kevin J., and Owen Strachan, *The Pastor as Public Theologian: Reclaiming a Lost Vision* (Grand Rapids, MI: Baker Academic, 2015).

Waters, Guy Prentiss, *How Jesus Runs the Church* (Phillipsburg, NJ: P & R Publishing, 2011).

Watson, David, *I Believe in the Church* (London: Hodder & Stoughton, 1978).

Wilson, Arthur L., and Ronald M. Cervero, 'Democracy and Program Planning', *New Directions for Adult & Continuing Education*, 128 (2010): 81-89.

Witmer, Timothy Z., *The Shepherd Leader: Achieving Effective Shepherding in Your Church* (Phillipsburg, NJ: P & R Publishing, 2010).

Woodhouse, John, *Unity That Helps & Unity That Hinders* (Sheffield: Reform, 2001).

If you have enjoyed this book, you might like to consider:

- supporting the work of the Latimer Trust
- reading more of our publications
- recommending them to others

See www.latimertrust.org for more information.

## Latimer Studies

## Anglican Foundations Series

| | | |
|---|---|---|
| BF | Being Faithful: The Shape of Historic Anglicanism Today | Theological Resource Group of GAFCON |
| TPG | The True Profession of the Gospel: Augustus Toplady and Reclaiming our Reformed Foundations | Lee Gatiss |
| SG | Shadow Gospel: Rowan Williams and the Anglican Communion Crisis | Charles Raven |
| TTB | Translating the Bible: From William Tyndale to King James | Gerald Bray |
| PWS | Pilgrims, Warriors, and Servants: Puritan Wisdom for Today's Church | ed. Lee Gatiss |
| PPA | Preachers, Pastors, and Ambassadors: Puritan Wisdom for Today's Church | ed. Lee Gatiss |
| CWP | The Church, Women Bishops and Provision: The Integrity of Orthodox Objections to the Proposed Legislation Allowing Women Bishops | |
| TSF | The Truth Shall Set You Free: Global Anglicans in the 21$^{st}$ Century | ed. Charles Raven |
| LMM | Launching Marsden's Mission: The Beginnings of the Church Missionary Society in New Zealand, viewed from New South Wales | eds. Peter G Bolt David B. Pettett |
| MST1 | Listen To Him: Reading and Preaching Emmanuel in Matthew | Ed. Peter Bolt |
| GWC | The Genius of George Whitefield: Reflections on his Ministry from 21$^{st}$ Century Africa | Ed. Benjamin Dean & Adriaan Neele |

CPSIA information can be obtained
at www.ICGtesting.com
Printed in the USA
BVHW081213261021
619917BV00009B/320